Sh[e]

An Spy During World War II

Jeane Slone

SHE WAS AN AMERICAN SPY DURING WORLD WAR II
© 2013 Jeane Slone

ISBN: 978-0-9838154-2-6

LCCN: 2013920003

Printed in the United States of America

Walter J. Willey Book Company

This historical novel is based entirely on fact. The characters have been fictionalized.

Acknowledgments

Writing this historical fiction took a small "army" of people in order to complete. I would like to thank...

Dennis Ness, Elizabeth Beryl Vedros, Sivani Lloyd, Mona Mechling, and Thomas J. Tessier for their sharp eyes in finding errors in the beginning manuscript.

Manuscripts To Go, Cris Wanzer, for her fine and enthusiastic professional help in editing and book design.

Elizabeth Vega for her "twin theory."

Amy Calhoun, spy web design.

Major Alan Edwards, Corps Historian, for a personal tour of The Military Intelligence Museum, Chicksands Military Base, Bedford, England.

Norcal Skydiving, Cloverdale, CA, where I had the opportunity to skydive.

John Boraggina, curator of the Santa Catalina Island Museum.

Paul Heck, Board of Directors, Pacific Coast Air Museum, Santa Rosa, CA, avid pilot and gun aficionado, for allowing me to practice shooting his father's WW II Colt .45 on Allan Morgan's acreage. (Past President of Pacific Coast Air Museum, Santa Rosa, CA.)

Technical Advisors

Thanks to David Harrison for his technical advice regarding wireless transmitters and giving me the opportunity to use his 1948 clandestine RS-1 HF transceiver. He is a technical advisor for wireless transmitters, active ham operator, former communications officer and judge advocate in the USAF, and former patent attorney.

Charley Taylor, for his glider knowledge and his research in military censorship. He is a retired Naval Aviator who flew the A-6 Intruder off the *USS Enterprise* in Vietnam. He is currently the Guest Speaker Coordinator at the Pacific Coast Air Museum in Santa Rosa, CA.

Margo VanVeen, for her assistance with the French language.

Vic Titoni, for reviewing the weapons parts in the manuscript, co-owner of Schmidt & Titoni Firearms & Accessories, 808 Piner Road, Santa Rosa, CA.

Contents

Acknowledgments iii

Preface ix

Chapter 1: Gliders 1

Chapter 2: Mother 7

Chapter 3: The Army 12

Chapter 4: Changes 17

Chapter 5: Secretarial Position 21

Chapter 6: An Interview 27

Chapter 7: Canada 33

Chapter 8: Camp X 40

Chapter 9: Basic Training 47

Chapter 10: Pretty Odd Fish 53

Chapter 11: Guns 58

Chapter 12: Parachuting 65

Chapter 13: Morse Code 69

Chapter 14: Machine Carbines 74

Chapter 15: A Mandatory Party 80

Chapter 16: A Good Friend 86

Chapter 17: A Uniform 93

Chapter 18: *USS Avalon* 98

Chapter 19: Santa Catalina Island 103

Chapter 20: Spies 110

Chapter 21: Vacation 116

Chapter 22: The Blimp 123

Chapter 23: Beaulieu, England 129

Chapter 24: Finishing School 137

Chapter 25: Biking Around the New Forest 142

Chapter 26: Jacqueline 147

Chapter 27: Letters 154

Chapter 28: Interrogation..159

Chapter 29: Missing..164

Chapter 30: Officer Vivian Armstrong.......................................169

Chapter 31: Mission Washington, DC...175

Chapter 32: The French Ambassador 181

Chapter 33: Ciphers..186

Chapter 34: A New Mission 189

Chapter 35: Tangmere 193

Chapter 36: Westland Lysander...199

Chapter 37: Occupied Paris 205

Chapter 38: Marie...210

Chapter 39: Escape 215

Chapter 40: Two Years Later 220

Epilogue…...223

Biographies of Real WW II Spies

Virginia Hall..227

Elizabeth Amy Thorpe (Betty Pack)...228

Noor Inayat Khan 229

Vera Atkins 231

Bibliography...232

About the Front Cover...235

About the Author...236

She Was
An American Spy
During World War II

PREFACE

There were very few American women spies during World War II. Women spies were looked upon as expendable. They received very little pay and no benefits. What they all shared was a strong, fierce conviction to end a long, arduous war. Many women watched their men risk their lives and they too wanted to do their patriotic duty to help end this war.

The bombing of Pearl Harbor ended our isolationism and the men joined the battle. Because women were regarded as expendable, they were taught everything the men were taught, from Jiu-jitsu to gunfighting, and all the tricks of espionage.

Chapter 1
Gliders

Glider school, of all things! I had assumed the school wouldn't accept my husband when he applied. After all, Fred didn't have the required college education to be a pilot, and had no flying experience whatsoever. It was the article in the *Rochester Times* that got him started on the idea. I sat in the kitchen and reread the article once again.

> *General Hap Arnold, the father of the U.S. Army glider program, has so far rounded up a fearless band of 5,000 volunteer aviators to bring infantry and vital supplies one-way into enemy territory. The program has been very successful and more troops are needed. A pilot's license is not required. Be a glider pilot in the U.S. Army. It's a he-man's job for men who want to serve their country in the air. Help our country soar to victory. See your Army recruitment office today!*

Fred told me Germany was the first country to use gliders, as far back as World War I. They had recently attacked Greece by sending in glider planes. Then, Britain saw the potential in gliders. Our isolationism was ended by Pearl Harbor, and we were thrown into the war. Now, two weeks after the bombing, General Arnold wanted 1,000 glider pilots.

After the news of Pearl Harbor, my twin brother Harry had enlisted immediately, angry over the Japanese attack. It only took my husband a short while to button up all the details at his bottle factory in order to join up, as well.

Fred and I had avidly followed the news of the war in Europe together. His pride of wanting to defend his country was a virtue to be admired, but the job seemed too dangerous to me. I was much too young to be a widow. I was under the impression that he was content being the owner of our large bottle factory. The thought of Fred gliding in a plane that had no motor, one-way into enemy territory, sounded extremely risky to me, and I felt this type of job would be better suited for a single man. Fred didn't share my concerns, nor did he seem to mind leaving me behind with the burden of my mother's care. Her failing health now required constant attention from me.

Within a few weeks, my anger over him leaving began to soften as I reflected on the past. After all, it had been Fred's generous idea to move Mother in with us after Dad had passed away the previous year following a sudden heart attack. It was almost as though the approach of another war was too much for my father to take. He had almost lost an arm serving in the infantry during WW I. When Mom called with the shocking news, Fred had held me tightly, rubbing my back with soothing comfort. He knew how close I was to my father.

In the beginning, Fred and I would both go off to work and come home to Mom, who made us dinner and a freshly baked pie each day. Then one day we opened the front door and the smell of burning cotton hit our noses. Fred hurried inside and we saw Mother sweeping the kitchen floor, the same spot over and over. In the next room was an ironing board with the iron flat down, smoking and burning one of my favorite blouses. Fred unplugged it, snapped up the singed blouse, and threw it into the sink of unwashed dishes.

"Oh my God, Mother! You could've burned the house down!" I reprimanded her, surprised by our role reversal.

She had a befuddled look on her face as she mumbled, "Wh-what?"

That event changed my life, and I had to quit my job as a secretary in Fred's factory. My concerned husband insisted that she should not be left alone, and he was right. Fred would leave for work and Mom would simply sit on the couch, staring into space.

I found her wicker basket of crocheting and placed it between us on the davenport. "I can't wait until you finish this bedspread, Mom. It will brighten up your bedroom." I placed a half-finished square on her lap with the metal hook in it.

Mom poked at it with one finger, staring down at our braided wool rug that we had once worked on together.

"I miss Dad, too," I said. "It's funny. What I miss about him most is his cigar smell. He put Harry and me to bed every night when we were kids and told us stories so you could clean up after dinner. Remember when he took us all to the lake in the summer every weekend?"

"Hmmm…" came from my mother's mouth as she closed her lips tight.

Sadness covered me like flies sticking to flypaper. I rose slowly and went to the kitchen to do the dishes. The olive green clock on the wall let me know I had four more hours until Fred got home. He knew how to draw Mother away from her blue moods. It was fun hearing them exchange puns back and forth, filling the house with joyful laughter.

The weeks of February crept by after Fred left for glider school, which was in the nearby town of Elmira, where the Elmira Area Soaring Corporation taught courses on glider flying for the Army. It might as well have been on the other side of the country since I couldn't visit him. My anger at being left alone with my mother began to overwhelm me without Fred coming home from work to relieve the boredom. Before Fred left for the service, he told me to do all my grocery shopping across the city at Mr. and Mrs. Andersen's store, instead of Mr. Taylor's, who was a single man. Fred always did have a jealous streak in him. At the glass factory, whenever any of the male workers greeted me he would look them up and down with suspicion and a snarl on his face.

I brewed a pot of coffee in the kitchen and poured it into one of my mother's fine patterned cups. Mom was on the sofa listening to the radio, which gave me time to study the new coupon book issued by the government. Thank goodness the *Rochester Times* article explained how to use the War Ration Coupon Book. I studied the instructions on the back of the tan-colored, 6 x 4-inch booklet:

> *This book is valuable. Do not lose it. Do not throw this book away when all of the stamps have been used or when the time for their use has expired. You may be required to present this book when you apply for subsequent books. Rationing is a vital part of your country's war effort. Any attempt to violate*

the rules is an effort to deny someone his share and will create hardship and help the enemy. This book is your government's assurance of your right to buy your fair share of certain goods made scarce by war. Price ceilings have also been established for your protection. Dealers must post these prices conspicuously. Don't pay more. Give your whole support to retaining and thereby conserve our vital goods. Be guided by the rules: "If you don't need it, DON'T BUY IT."

In the far right corner of the booklet was a warning statement:

This book is the property of the United States Government. It is unlawful to sell it to any other person, or to use it or permit anyone else to use it, except to obtain rationed goods in accordance to the regulations of the Office of Price Administration. Any person who finds a lost War Ration Book must return it to the War Price and Rationing Board, which issued it. Persons who violate rationing regulations are subject to a $10,000 fine or imprisonment, or both.

With care, I wrote my name and age on the booklet: Kathleen Dwyer, 26 years old. I hesitated, then wrote my weight and height on the front cover. I was proud of my figure, but it was no one's business what my measurements were, especially a storekeeper's. I bit my pencil and examined each page. The tiny stamps with pictures of Army tanks and airplanes were quite adorable, but the 48 points allotted each month to buy certain foods did not seem like a sufficient amount.

"Oh, darn," I said out loud as I examined the diagram labeled "Points on Most Popular Cans." After doing the math, I discovered that if I were to buy three cans of peas it would use up all my points for the entire month. I squeezed the back of my neck.

Between the money Dad had left and the income from Fred's factory, we were well off, unlike many other families. Unfortunately, everyone got the same amount of points, whether rich or poor. This complicated rationing business would make for a long war, and I hoped I could manage. The best activity I could find to escape my humdrum life was shopping.

I glanced over at Mother after hearing her random mumbles. She was sitting in her usual spot on the sofa sorting torn, tan pieces of paper over and over again, whispering to herself in English, then in her native French.

"Why am I still here? *Pourquoi?*" she pleaded in her thin, shaky voice.

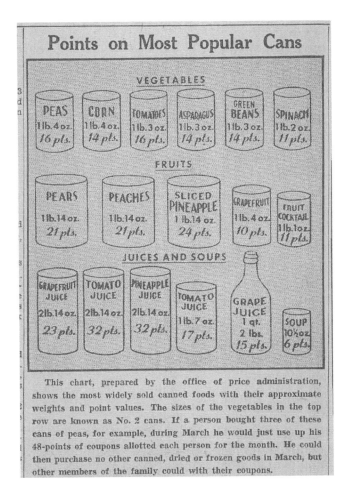

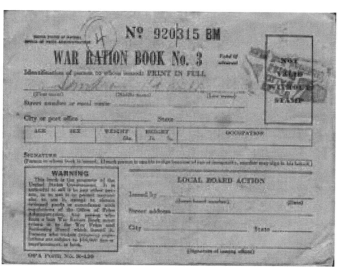

Chapter 2
Mother

I found myself missing Fred. He had been a strong buffer against the disagreements I began having with my rapidly aging mother. She wasn't that old, but since Dad's death, she acted so feeble, instead of like the staunch French aristocrat I was used to. I couldn't help but feel resentful that I had to quit my job at the factory, but after the iron incident, there was no choice. She had to be watched. My feelings fluctuated between being upset with her to feeling sorry for her.

After sweeping the kitchen floor, I heard Mother mumble in the next room, "When am I going to go?"

I went into the living room. "Mom, we've gone over this subject before. Try to keep busy. Here, read the *Saturday Evening Post*."

After placing the magazine on her lap, I tried to take the scraps of paper from her hands. She gripped them and put them under the magazine, then settled back on the sofa, flipping the pages. Her finger began to underline each word as she squinted her eyes. I went into her bedroom and searched around for her eyeglasses, then hurried back to the living room. I watched her struggling with the words again. I placed the glasses on her face, sat down, and read her one of the articles.

Mother patted my lap after I was done. "Thank you, dear."

I put a radio show on for her while I went to do the dishes. The episode of "The Adventures of the Thin Man" was enthralling, and I kept the clatter down as I washed the soapy plates.

"When am I going to go?" shouted Mother above the mysterious music.

Her constant repetition was getting on my nerves, and I gnawed on the side of my lip. I didn't want her to "go" and did love my mother, but my patience was dissipating as the days wore on. Since Dad died, my refined, educated mother was getting wackier by the month. Oh, how I missed being able to discuss this problem with Fred. I had not received even one letter since he left. Fred used to come home from work, give me a perfunctory kiss, then settle right down next to my mother to attempt a conversation with her. I was then able to go off into the bedroom for some alone time, either to polish my nails or brush my hair while listening to a show. The news on the radio from the outside world alleviated my closeted existence. Maybe I would get a letter from Fred today, or perhaps from my brother.

I had just hung my apron on a doorknob in the hall when Mom said once again, "Kathleen, why am I still here?"

I smiled upon hearing my name this time. "Mom, I have to walk into town to get groceries. Do you need anything?"

I needed to get out for a short break, and hoped she wouldn't ask to come. It took too much patience on my part to walk as slow as she did. I timed my departure during her favorite program, "Ozzie and Harriet," hoping she wouldn't get up and get into anything until it was over.

"Don't buy me green bananas, in case the Good Lord does take me today."

I put on my winter hat and coat. She went back to the magazine, penciling under each word as the laughter rose from the radio. I kissed her wrinkled cheek.

"Have a nice time, dear," she called out as I left.

Every shop window seemed to display less and less each week because of the shortages. I lingered in front of each one on the way to the store. In the reflection in one of the windows, I turned from side to side, but stopped when I noticed a few stray Army rejects leering at my large breasts beneath my thin coat. You'd think I'd be used to it by now. I buttoned up a few buttons to make my chest look a little flatter—as if that were possible. Some women were blessed with an adequate bust, but mine was enormous and far too large for my small frame. It was almost a handicap, and gave me back pain at times.

Mr. Taylor looked up from his newspaper as the bell rang when I entered the store.

"Hello there, Mrs. Dwyer. Nice weather we're having this winter." His eyes drifted to my breasts.

"Yes, I hope we don't get any more snow this year. Nice bow tie," I flirted, hoping he would help me with my coupons.

He straightened his tie and looked at my legs. "You're lucky to have silk stockings to wear."

"I only have one more pair, I'm afraid. I know there won't be any more available with the way this war is escalating." I looked back at my legs and straightened the seams, knowing he was watching me.

Mr. Taylor pointed to a wooden bin in the corner of his store. "After you wear them out, you can bring them here. All the storekeepers are collecting them for the war effort."

Above the bin a sign was hung that read:

Uncle Sam needs your discarded silk and nylon stockings
for gunpowder bags. Please launder and leave here!

He stared at me again. I moved away as Fred crept into my mind. I found some semi-ripe bananas, a loaf of bread, and a few cans of vegetables, and put them on the counter.

I flipped and fumbled through the pages of the ration booklet.

Mr. Taylor took it. "Here, I'll help you with the stamps." He thumbed through the booklet, carefully tore the stamps out in the proper direction, then placed a small, dark red coin and a bright blue coin in my hand. He saw my questioning face and explained that they were change coins for the ration stamps.

I felt the itty-bitty coins, smaller than dimes, in the palm of my hand. On each side it said "OPA RED POINT" and "OPA BLUE POINT," then the number one was displayed in the center.

"They're cute, thanks!"

"You betcha!" he exclaimed, winking.

I inched down the block as slowly as possible to avoid the long day ahead at home. Sometimes guilt and a deep sadness crept upon me whenever Mom asked, "Why am I still here?" I felt pity. I knew all she wanted was to be with Dad. After all, they had passed their anniversary when he had his heart attack.

It made me wonder, where was my resilient, intelligent mother? I missed the mother who had strong opinions on every subject. I missed the way she loved to share her wealth of knowledge about Europe and her native country of France. As soon as I had learned to write in school, she would sit up close and show me the lovely, written French language. I would breathe in her divine perfume, *Guerlain*. She spoke to me most of the time in French, so I was bilingual at quite a young age. My brother, Harry, picked up on the language also, but never absorbed it as well as I did. If it hadn't been for her insistence that I go to the Sorbonne University in Paris, I would never have received a degree in French Literature. I felt very lucky to have had the opportunity to advance my education in the heavenly city of Paris. We were all going to take a vacation there together until Dad got sick and passed away.

Mother used to recite French poems and songs to me. Where her vocabulary was once immense, now all she could repeat were the same phrases over and over. My heart broke a little each day. I felt so sad that her feeble mind had replaced her once sharp, lucid intellect. It was as if part of her had left with Dad and now she bided her time, waiting to go to the forever resting place where he had gone.

Chapter 3
The Army

U pon returning home, I reached inside the mailbox, shuffled through the bills, then tore open a letter from Fred.

Kathleen, my dearest:

The glider school is a dream come true for me. Although I enjoyed being in charge of production at the factory, pilot training expands my education while challenging my ability to learn a new, valuable skill. I am proud to be part of this fledgling aviation program. Right here on Harris Hill in Elmira, the first national soaring contest was held in 1930. The updraft from its ridge makes Harris Hill a naturally suited environment for glider flight. I love soaring above the Chemung River Valley with its majestic hills and deep glens. There truly is no better way to take in the breathtaking beauty of New York's Finger Lakes Region than from the cockpit of a glider!

How is Mother and how is your patience holding out?

Please write soon and send me some of your wonderful oatmeal cookies that I dream about.

Love as always, Fred

The letter from Fred gave me a basket of mixed emotions. His concern about my mother brought a warm smile upon my face, but I couldn't help but have a tinge of jealousy. Life was getting very dull. When I was a secretary at our factory, I enjoyed my job and was reluctant to quit to take care of Mom. If I had gotten pregnant before Fred left, it would have helped keep my mind off the monotony. But then, we rarely had sex. Fred always said he was tired all the time. I knew he was attracted to my figure as much as any other man, but he couldn't function very often and made excuses. Fred almost didn't make the cutoff age of 35 to qualify for the Army glider school. He kept telling me it was his last chance in life for an adventure.

A week later, I announced to Mother, "I'm going to the store. We're out of bread." I glanced at the clock on the china hutch, knowing her radio program was about to begin.

She answered in a full sentence. "I'm coming with you this time, Kathleen."

"Mom, the store is too far for you to walk. I won't be gone long." I opened the closet to get my coat.

"I have two legs, don't I? You need me to help carry the groceries from the store, don't you?"

Surprised at hearing several complete sentences, I countered, "I only need bread. Besides, it's very windy out. Stay here and listen to the radio so you don't miss your favorite show."

"I need soup. You never get soup."

"Okay," I answered in a weak voice. I was quite worried about her walking that far, but I needed her ration book anyway, since I was running low on coupons. "Mom, where's your ration coupon book?"

"What's that, dear?"

I sighed and went rummaging through her bureau. The color tan flashed through my mind. I dashed into the living room. I tried to pry up the sofa cushion next to her, but Mother held it down. I pulled the cushion away from her, and underneath it I found the ration coupon booklet, all torn up.

"Mother, why did you do this?" I grabbed the torn pieces, then threw them down on the rug. They scattered about in shreds.

"What's the matter, darling?" Her innocent voice softened me while she picked up some of the pieces and tried to straighten them into a

13

booklet again.

I stomped out of the room. Now we would both have to share one book for the entire month. I hoped that Mr. Taylor would be in a chipper mood, and would let me buy more food if I gave him a tip. It was annoying to have the money and not be allowed to buy all that I wanted. Sugar stamps were good for a total of five pounds for two months, and then expired.

I must ask Mother to stop using so much sugar in her tea and on her Cornflakes. I must conserve the sugar, also, I thought. After all, I needed to bake cookies, or at least cornbread, to mail to Fred at the pilot school.

I flipped through my ration book to calculate how many points I had left. "Mom, I'll get your favorite Campbell's chicken noodle soup. I'll only be gone a short while," I told her.

"I...I want different...I need to see what they have at the store." She pushed up from the arm of the couch and tottered to the hall closet.

I felt exasperated and went into the bedroom. My silk stockings in the thin red box were protected by tissue paper. I lifted them out and slipped a hand into one. Feeling a tiny run, I got out my bottle of nail varnish and put a red dot on it, hoping it would stop the run from getting bigger. These were probably going to be the last pair I would have until the war ended.

When I came out of the bedroom, Mother had replaced her housedress with a nice print one. I hadn't seen her in a decent dress in weeks. Her coat was draped on her arm. I helped her put it on. I noticed her outdated hat. I searched through the closet and pulled out one of mine instead. She tried to shake it off her head until I held my long-handled mirror up to her face. My burgundy velvet hat with the wide brim brought out the sparkle in her blue eyes.

Mother beamed. "Why, I do look attractive." She cocked her head to the side and felt the brim.

"My hat suits you very well."

As we walked to the store, Mother shuffled behind me, stopping and pointing at every shop window along the way. I gently put my arm through hers. I was never one to stroll and preferred brisk walking.

When we entered the grocery store, I called out in a cheerful voice, "Hello, Mr. Taylor."

"How are you today, Mrs. Dwyer? Why, Mrs. Carlson, I haven't seen you in quite a while."

His eyes were riveted on my blouse. I closed up my coat.

"Well, I'm still here, aren't I?" Mom shook her finger at him while my face flushed.

"Indeed you are! What a stunning hat."

"My daughter doesn't let me out very often." She looked down and twiddled her thumbs.

I turned away and went to see if there was any bread. Mother tried to follow me, shuffling up and down each aisle. She would stop, point, then mumble, move a few inches and start again. I got the several items I came for and put them on the counter, then went back to find her. Mother held a soup can in her hand, looked at the price, shook her head, and put it back.

"Why don't you get it, Mom? This is why you came."

"Too much!" she shouted.

I whispered, lying, "It's on sale. It really costs less."

I scooped it up and placed it on the counter with the other food. I found the right coupons, and paid Mr. Taylor the two dollars and 50 cents that he announced. By then, I had forgotten about flirting with him to avoid using the few stamps I had left. I looped my arm through my mother's, got the bag, then left when she switched half her sentence to French.

After the long trek home, I placed the cans of soup on the top shelf in the kitchen cabinet and settled into the rocking chair to read a letter that I had gotten from Harry.

> *Dear Sis:*
> *I hope you are coping with the care of our mother. Even*
> *though I am only 10 minutes older than you, I need to give*

you some advice. I could sense by your last letter that caring for Mom is not an easy job. Try to put yourself in her shoes. She misses Dad as much as you do, but cannot find the words to tell you. Try to keep her busy and take her places. This will lift her spirits more. Also, have patience and sympathy toward her. Remember how much fun you both had together going to the opera and plays? She was the one who insisted on us both taking those expensive piano lessons, not Dad.

I am shipping out to an island on the Pacific Coast called Santa Catalina. It is actually a part of California. I'll write after I settle in there.

Your "older" brother, Harry

I threw the letter into my top dresser drawer in my room and pushed it in so fast that the drawer clattered.

Mom called, "What happened, dear?"

I ignored her, lost in thought. *Harry is so bossy. If he could take a turn babysitting Mom, he would see how hard it is. I need something to do…or at least some alone time.*

Chapter 4
Changes

Several weeks crawled by like ants in search of water on a hot day. I was able to escape for the occasional short walk to the park. From the bench I watched with a longing while two children giggled, swinging high into the air on the park swing set. My mind drifted toward Fred. I gazed up at the puffy clouds that dotted the blue sky. His attentiveness toward Mom only satisfied me part of the time. I needed him to be physically more affectionate toward me. I sighed and retrieved his latest letter from my coat pocket.

> *Kathleen, my dearest:*
>
> *This glider flying program has been quite intense, but I am thrilled to be able to fly a motorless aircraft that is released by a tow-rope. I qualified for my first solo flight here at the Elmira Area Soaring Corporation. By completing my eight hours, I can now pilot a Waco tug plane. You would be so proud of me. The scenery is quite beautiful from the sky over Elmira. We have been lucky to have such a mild winter to train in with very little snowfall. The CG-4A I have been practicing in as a co-pilot can seat a troop of 15 soldiers (this includes two pilots) and costs the Army over $15,000! Two pilots sit side by side while we are towed at a maximum safe speed of 150 miles per hour. Our tow-rope is hooked to a powered airplane. When we reach a certain height, I pull a handle that unhooks the rope. Gravity pulls the glider down and rising air creates lift that pushes the glider up, then the*

plane glides on its own. A glider stays in the sky by flying between updrafts and thermals. (Thermals are areas of heated air that rise.) We have a lot of updrafts here in Elmira because we are surrounded by hills, and the wind is forced up when it hits a hill or mountain.

Our CG-4A has a reputation of being the most forgiving, ugly beast ever flown. Its wingspan is 83.6 feet, with a length of 48 feet. It is hard to imagine that it is capable of carrying 4,060 pounds, which is 620 more pounds than the glider's own empty weight! The entire nose section (including the pilot's compartment) swings upward for rapid loading and unloading of an assortment of heavy items like jeeps, radio equipment, combat supplies, and even a small bulldozer. The world record for the longest distance a glider has ever flown is 1,900 miles and took 15 hours!

I miss you every day and hope you are coping with caring for your mother. I know how hard it has been for you since your father died. Have you heard from your brother Harry? I wonder where he is stationed now?

Write and wish me luck on my cross-country solo flight. I am honored to be in this training program to fly this magnificent plane and serve my country.

Best to Mother,

Love as always, Fred

The children's laughter carried my mood gaily upward. After reading Fred's letter, I worried about his safety, but felt proud of his commitment to the Army. He loved me so much that this reflection brought a sweet smile to my face and I skipped home.

It was quiet when I opened the front door. I peered into the living room, then dashed into the kitchen. There sprawled upon the floor was Mom, face down, her dress hiked up to her waist and her petticoat showing.

"Oh, my God!" I screamed, seeing the footstool lying on its side near the cabinet. I grabbed the phone in the hall. After dialing, I yelled, "Operator, send an ambulance! My mother has had an accident."

After I gave the address and hung up, I bent down and touched her forehead. Relief swept over me when I heard her thin voice.

"I fell...fell."

The first visit to the hospital was promising. Mother attempted to explain to me that she had slipped while trying to reach for a new can of soup. The doctor informed me that she had broken a hip and she might recover, but slowly.

At home I sat in the kitchen, staring into space and playing the "should've game" over and over. I should've prepared her lunch before leaving for the park. I should not have put the soup up so high...

Upon the next visit to the hospital, the nurse told me Mother was not eating. I pleaded with her and tried to spoon some Jell-O into her mouth. Every day I went and visited Mom, trying to feed her a variety of hospital food, but she remained stubborn and turned her head away.

The phone rang a week later at 3:30 in the morning, waking me from a night of tossing and turning. The nurse said she was sorry. Sorry? Why was the nurse sorry? She didn't even know my mother. I hung up and stared into the darkness. My body was numb. I hugged my nightgown and slouched down on the rocker.

I anticipated Fred's arrival for the funeral, hoping he could comfort me. Harry made it from California shortly thereafter.

My brother confided in me after Fred went to get the newspaper.

"She was a wonderful mother, Kitty, and I know at the end it was hard for you."

He called me "Kitty," like Dad used to.

A tear dribbled down my cheek. "Yes, Harry, she was a good mother to us," I choked out.

Harry reached over and held my hand, renewing our closeness as only twins could experience.

At the funeral, I clung to Fred, burying my face in the smell of his Army uniform. He stroked my hair when the pastor said, "Ashes to ashes…"

I looked into my husband's face and saw that his eyes were also filled with tears. He was such a kind, sensitive man, and I felt blessed to be married to him.

That night, I desperately snuggled up to Fred. He kissed my forehead, whispering, "Try to get some sleep, honey."

I reached down to arouse him, but he pulled away. "Not now. Your brother will hear."

I rolled away, crunched myself into a ball, and hugged my breasts tightly as silent tears moistened my pillow. I remembered how many times he had said that when Mother was in the next bedroom.

Chapter 5
Secretarial Position

After my husband and brother returned to duty, I found myself happy to be alone. It was a release and sense of freedom to not have the responsibility of my mother's care. Then, as time went by, guilt seeped into every aspect of my being, both when I was awake and in my dreams. Scenes would run through my mind over and over: I made a nice lunch for Mom before I went out, discussing with her pleasant items to eat. I dreamed that I never left her alone and took her everywhere I could.

I found that keeping busy was the key to preventing myself from feeling distraught. I read the entire *Rochester Times* every day with a big pot of percolated coffee brewing on the stove. First, there were all the reports of the war, which I avidly followed to stay informed in order to find something to write to Fred about. I glanced at the map of the world pinned to the kitchen wall to study each foreign country the newspaper would mention. I saved the funnies page for last, and enjoyed finding out what Dick Tracy was up to.

My eyes wandered over the want ads as I sipped hot coffee from one of Mom's fancy cups. Most of the jobs were to join a branch of the service or work in factory war production. It was good Fred had hired a competent manager to take over his factory while he was in the service. *I suppose I could go back there and work*, I thought. Then a wonderful opportunity popped out at me.

Wanted: Secretary able to type 65 WPM
Fluency in European languages a must

Pay $300-$400 a month
Reply: Overseas Supply Service
277 5th St., New York, New York

The pay seemed high for a secretarial position. The typing was not what excited me, though I was certain I was qualified for the job. My speed had been above average when I worked in the factory, and I was sure it was still almost up to par. The fluency in a European language, now that's what whetted my appetite. Here was my chance to serve my country and end this boredom of waiting for Fred to come home.

I wrote to the address in the ad and waited impatiently for a reply. My large library collection of French books from the university had come in handy at last. I studied them with diligence. Over the next few days, I thumbed through some old French children's books. Fond memories of my mother flooded over me as I went through the many battered copies. *Bécassine* was my favorite. In my best French accent I read aloud the story. At last, good thoughts were replacing the guilt I had been feeling after Mother passed away. I realized now that she had spent far more time with me than Harry. Mom had taught me French, and the geography of Europe, grooming me to be accepted into Sorbonne University. I knew she had longed to go to this university herself when she was young, but her family had sent her two older brothers, instead.

A week later I received an application. The part that seemed odd to me was where it said to list addresses and phone numbers of all relatives and friends. In bold letters it stated: *Do not leave anyone off the list.*

Hmmm, I thought. *This must be a new wartime protocol.*

I mailed it back and waited again. Life began to agitate me once more. The waiting game—for Fred, for my brother, for the war to end, and now for a job interview.

The next day over coffee I read a frightening article about glider planes.

DIGNITARIES DEAD FROM
GLIDER PLANE ACCIDENT

A new CG-4A glider plane manufactured by the Robertson Aircraft Corporation was delivered to the Lambert Field Airport in St. Louis. Many officials gathered in celebration to volunteer to go for a ride to express their patriotic support of the factory workers.

The St. Louis dignitaries that boarded the glider included: the mayor, judges, Chamber of Commerce presidents, the president of Robertson Aircraft, and various Army personnel. Several thousand people gathered for this festive event with a full military band.

An airplane climbed to 3,000 feet with the glider in tow and passed over the airport crowds as they waved and cheered.

Captain Klugh hit the glider release lever above his head and the tow-line fell away. The CG-4A rose a few feet in the air and then began to descend. The crowd heard a loud cracking noise, like a thunderbolt. The right wing had shot violently upward and broken off, causing it to nosedive straight into the tarmac at 80 miles per hour. Everyone aboard was instantly killed.

At first, statements came out that it was sabotage by enemy agents causing the wing to tear away from the glider. A thorough investigation revealed that the Robertson Company did not manufacture the wing according to the specifications of the military. The wing was not thick enough, making it a defective part.

This has not been the first accident involving a glider plane. Last month, there was another crash in Tennessee where several passengers were killed.

The public is asking: Can the big, fully loaded CG-4As land troops and equipment in rough fields and farm pastures *safely?*

General Arnold has commanded the War Department to set up centralized schools for quality control inspectors.

My hand shook as I clipped out the newspaper article and shoved it into an envelope. With it, I enclosed a long note to Fred expressing my panic. This was a CG-4A accident, the same glider plane type that my husband was piloting.

The return letter from Fred did little to ease my concerns. He wrote that General Hap Arnold was doing everything possible in order for his "pet project" to succeed. Many inspectors came to the Elmira Soaring School and reinspected the CG-4As. All of the gliders passed with flying colors. Fred wrote that General Arnold stated that he expected a glider force that was second to none.

My dreams that night consisted of watching Fred soaring above Harris Hill. I heard his glider wing crack off and spent the rest of the war crying at the kitchen table. Sweat was on my forehead, and drool spread across the pillow as I awoke with a throbbing headache.

Two weeks went by, and at last a letter from the job I applied for arrived.

Overseas Supply Service
477 5th St.
Office 12
New York, New York
April 20, 1942

Dear Mrs. Kathleen Dwyer:
Your application qualifies you for an interview. Come to the above address at 1 p.m., Thursday April 27, 7th Floor, room 12.

Do not disclose this address or any information about the interview or you will be automatically disqualified.

I read the brief letter over again. This spurred me to practice on my Underwood in case there would be a typing test. With a fury I tapped away, while my mind wandered to my upcoming trip to New York City.

An interview in New York City! I hadn't been to the big city since I was a young child. It was quite far from Rochester. My parents had taken me to a Broadway play as a present for my 16th birthday. Everything was very grand in the spectacular playhouse with the glamorous costumes the actors wore. I could still sing the songs from *Girl Crazy*, but of course I could never hold a note for 16 measures like Ethel Merman did.

The last line of the letter demanded secrecy. I chewed on a broken fingernail and decided it must be a job helping with the war effort.

I had to take a bus in the middle of the night from Rochester in order to get to the appointment on time. There was very little choice as to which bus to take since the war began. The seven-hour ride wasn't too bad. I slept most of the time.

When I got off the bus, I waited on the cold, open platform for the 10:52 morning train. The clickety-clack sound and rocking motion of the train soothed me, but also invigorated me. Then it became obnoxious. The Army troops made the trip congested, as well as pungent. Several of the uniformed men bumped into my breasts on purpose. I was able to find a window seat to huddle up to, buffering myself from the boyish snickering.

Two subways later, I walked down five long city blocks at a fast pace to make the interview on time. The address was in the heart of the buzzing city.

An old, brown-gray building had number 477 on it. I double-checked it on my letter and took the creaky elevator up to the seventh floor. The elevator was noisy, stopping and starting like my heartbeat. Would it break down? The light landed on number seven with a ding. I got out, took a deep breath, straightened my weary traveling clothes and wished I could find a restroom in order to fix my hair and make-up. It was dark and musty in the narrow hallway and I had to squint at the numbers on each door, looking for the right one.

There was room 12. I hesitated for a moment, nervous about the whole event. Upon opening the door, I entered a small, unkempt, dusty office. It was dim and plain. I wondered if I even wanted to work there. The musty smell wrinkled up my nose. A matronly looking woman behind a small desk looked me over and told me to have a seat. There was only one old chair in the entire room other than hers. She went into a back office, then returned and resumed writing on stacks of papers. I fidgeted with the buttons on my coat and pulled at my stockings. After 15 minutes I got up and took off my coat, my face flushed from the overheated room.

Chapter 6
An Interview

A smallish man stormed out of the back office. His beady eyes looked me over with suspicion. "Follow me," he announced. The room was the size of a closet, cluttered with boxes piled on top of each other. There were no windows, which gave it a moldy smell mixed with tobacco.

Without any greeting, he began the first round of questions while puffing on a cigarette. He tapped the ashes into an overflowing metal tray, sometimes missing it altogether.

"So, Mrs. Dwyer, what languages do you speak?" His finger remained on my name on the application as if he might forget it.

"I can speak French fluently and took a year of Italian in school."

"What school did you go to?"

"It's on my application, the Sorbonne University in Paris." I pulled at the hem of my skirt.

"Aha!"

My eyes widened.

"What is the longest job you've held?"

"I worked for two years in a factory as a secretary." My hands squeezed tight, knuckles bulging.

While firing a barrage of questions at me, the interviewer watched every move of my lips, eyes, and hands. Never once did he ask about my duties at the factory.

After the rapid deluge of questions, it made me wonder why he didn't read my application—all the answers were right there. This was a secretarial job, wasn't it?

I glanced over at a crooked war poster on the dingy wall that read: *Know Yourself...Know Your Weapon...Know Your Enemy.*

Quite suddenly the interviewer spoke in French. "How is the weather in Rochester? Tell me about it."

"*Pas mal,* at least it didn't snow on Easter this year," I answered as flawlessly as possible in a clipped pace, hoping it would hide any possible errors.

"Do you have a diary or have you ever written in one?"

"*Non,*" I answered, becoming agitated, wondering if he was testing my French or being nosy.

"Have you ever had a physical education class?" He switched back to English.

"*Oui,* tennis," I sighed, hoping I was using the right language this time.

"Can you cope with unusual situations?" he probed, lighting a new cigarette with the old one.

I thought, *You mean like this one?* But still wanting a job, I answered, "I think so," in French.

"Have you ever been overweight?" He glanced at my bust.

Now he was getting too personal. "Mr., uh…" I never was told his name. "…what do these questions have to do with typing?" I glanced over at the war poster again and asked, "Is this a war job?"

He loosened his tie. "Mrs. Dwyer, I'm the one who asks the questions. That is, if you still want the position. The receptionist will now give you a series of written intelligence tests. These will give me a general index of your capabilities and aptitudes. If you pass the tests, then I might answer your questions."

With pursed lips I glanced up at the dirty brown, cracked ceiling and suppressed a sigh.

He got up, his back to me, and went through his filing cabinet. After waiting a few minutes, he swung around to face me. "Mrs. Dwyer, my secretary is waiting for you."

I left his office. The secretary motioned for me to sit down and handed me the aptitude tests. I had to share her desk in order to fill them out. They consisted of translating languages. One page was in German and I only knew a few words. My eyes stung from being tired. I rubbed them, and tried to do my best. I glanced at the frumpy woman, wishing she would offer me a cup of coffee, but there was none in sight within the bare room. I finished all the tests and handed them in.

"All right, Mrs. Dwyer, you will be notified by mail in a few weeks if you pass the tests and the security check." The secretary stapled all the pages together.

At that point I lost my composure. "What? A security check for a shipping company secretary?"

She looked down at the papers and drummed her fingers. "If you pass the investigation check on all your relatives and acquaintances, we will call you in for a second interview."

"Investigation?" I pressed.

"Look, Miss, if you want the job this is the way it is," she whispered, looking toward her boss's door.

I sat there with my mouth open for a moment, then got up to leave.

The secretary went back to her papers, looked up, and surprised me by saying, "Thank you for coming in."

I left the mysterious office and mumbled, "Goodbye."

After the long trip back, I slept in the next morning. I took my coffee out into the warm air to retrieve the mail. It was a treat to hear a variety of birds announcing the arrival of spring. I read Fred's letter with hunger.

> *Kathleen, my dearest:*
> *I could sense by your last letter how worried you have been about me because of the glider plane mishaps. Enclosed is a newspaper article about Major Michael C. Murphy for you to read, to ease your concerns.*
> *Also, now that Major Murphy has proven gliders to be*

safe, there are 18 glider schools across the States.

Did you hear that students from Greenville High School in Michigan raised $72,000 and donated it to the Army Air Force to buy four gliders?

Thank you for the wonderful cornbread. I shared it with all my buddies.

Will write more when I have time.

Love as always,

Fred

Elmira Times

GLIDERS DECLARED SAFE TO HELP THE WAR EFFORT

There has been a recent series of accidents involving CG-4A glider planes, placing the important Army program in jeopardy. Major Michael C. Murphy organized a spectacular night-landing demonstration at an airfield in North Carolina for glider planes. The major is best known for his barnstorming aerobatics and is the first pilot in the world to take off and land an airplane on a moving automobile.

General Hap Arnold, along with other dignitaries, witnessed a surprise night-landing demonstration. Right before sunset, Major Murphy lectured to the VIPs as 10 Waco CG-4As touched down silently right behind them. The entire group turned around when they heard a nine-piece military band parade out of the uplifted nose of one of the gliders.

Major Murphy staged quite a show, proving that fully loaded combat gliders could make accurate and safe landings, even in total darkness, without the "enemy" finding out. The event's success breathed new life into the general's fledgling glider program, ensuring continued use to win the war.

The letter from Fred and the newspaper article somewhat eased my previous tension, though I still felt deep worry about my husband flying around in an aircraft that had no motor.

Two weeks dragged by, and I tried to adjust to the boredom of my life once again. I tuned into one of my favorite radio programs, "The Jack Benny Show," to pass the time. I chuckled every time he used his famous, exasperated expression, "Well!"

I opened a new bottle of nail varnish, and tried out a lighter shade of red this time.

A knock came at the door, startling me. I opened it a crack, wondering if perhaps it was my brother home on leave.

A Western Union carrier was there. "Name please?"

"Kathleen Dwyer."

He handed me a beige telegram.

"One minute." I went inside to get my purse. I gave him a tip and shut the door.

I sat down, paused, and closed my eyes before opening the telegram, wondering if it was about Fred being in a terrible accident. But, right at the top was the shipping company's address.

On 5/20 proceed to Toronto, Canada
Bring clothes in a single suitcase
Go to Royal York Hotel
Between the hours of 3-4 p.m. you will get a message with a number on it at front desk.
It will indicate the license plate on a vehicle you will ride in to get to your second interview.
Tell no one or you will automatically be disqualified from employment.

My hand quivered. I folded the telegram on the kitchen table and closed my eyes to steady my nerves. I picked it up again and reread it. Would I be crazy to go for this second interview? *This is absurd. I should write and discuss this with Fred*, I thought, but the last sentence, *tell no one or you will automatically be disqualified,* rang like an alarm in my head. Again, I thought, *All this secrecy for a secretarial job? Maybe the Overseas Supply Service is some sort of top-secret war operation.* This thought, whether true or not, eased my mind and did stir my sense of adventure. One suitcase meant I wouldn't be there very long. I had never been to Canada, even though Rochester was straight across Lake Ontario. I loved that huge, glassy lake and had strolled upon its shores many times. One week was all I had to figure out what to bring. Too bad I didn't have any stockings that were acceptable enough to wear. The long trip for my first interview had ruined my last pair.

Chapter 7
Canada

T he three-hour bus ride to Canada was scenic as the budding trees of spring rolled by my window. I was happy I had worn my smart, man-tailored suit because it never wrinkled.

The bus stopped right in front of the famous Royal York Hotel. Upon disembarking, I stood in front of the grand hotel, taking it all in. Huge fountains spouted water into the air. Manicured bushes landscaped the front with rows of ordered flowers placed between them. It was all so enchanting. I was pleased that I had worn my henna, rust-colored, high-crowned felt hat, which was fashionable-looking when placed on either side of my head, and still allowed my curls to show.

I walked to the front entrance and the uniformed doorman pulled open the heavy door for me. He stated in a charming, Canadian accent, "Welcome to the Royal York Hotel, Madame."

As I entered, I was mesmerized by the elegance surrounding me. I couldn't believe I was standing in the lobby of Canada's largest and newest hotel. The opulent, grand chandeliers twinkled brightly. I stared at the stunning, sweeping staircase going endlessly upward, making me wonder how many floors this hotel contained. There were fountains inside the lobby identical to those outside, but smaller. The melodious sound of the water gave me a calm feeling, even though there were many people bustling about.

I approached the expansive front desk, gripped my bag, and moistened my lips.

"Do you have reservations, Madame?" the handsome concierge

asked. His burgundy uniform with blue-gray piping around the collar gave him an air of authority. His sleeves bore military-looking stripes.

I swallowed and managed to give him a coquettish smile. "I'm expecting to receive a message between three and four o'clock here, but I think I'm early. Could you give me the time, please?"

He slipped out a gold-chained watch from one of his pockets and flipped it open, declaring, "It is 2:15. Name please?"

"What?"

"Madame, you said you were expecting a message."

"Oh, yes, sorry. Miss Dwyer," tumbled out of my mouth, as I wondered why I said "Miss."

The concierge turned his back and looked through a series of wooden slats. "No message, sorry." His smile broadened.

"I'm a bit early. I'll wander around and come back in a little while."

"I'd be happy to give you a tour of our gardens. Mr. Jacobs, please take over for me," he called over to the clerk, not giving me a moment to object.

The concierge came out from behind the large, circular counter and put his gloved hand through my arm. "Name's Martin Fairclough. Welcome to the Royal York Hotel. I'm happy to give you the grand tour." He took my suitcase and put it behind the counter before I could say another word.

My eyes twinkled as I realized why I had said "Miss." He was so darned good-looking and I could sense he liked my appearance, as well.

"This way to our gardens."

"Thank you. This is the most elegant hotel I have ever seen."

"Where are you from?" he asked, holding the weighty door to the outside.

"I'm from Rochester, New York, across the border."

"You have a wonderful accent."

"I was thinking the same of yours." I changed my hat to a prettier angle and pulled my cotton gloves up higher.

The gardens were similar to those at the front of the hotel, but on a grander scale. Abundant flowers spilled over every available space. The only type I could identify were the tulips, and they were in almost every color. All of the trees were trimmed with obvious care. A sharply cut maze of curved hedges surrounded us. Birds sang, flitting about, splashing in the decorated birdbaths.

"This is quite a magnificent garden."

"It's three acres and we employ seven gardeners to keep it in proper order."

"It's all very extraordinary. Could you tell me the time again, please?"

His shiny pocket watch glittered in the sun. "It is 2:30. We have enough time for me to show you one of the rooms."

"I'd love that. I was wondering what they looked like."

We went back inside and passed by a large concert hall. The concierge opened the door, pointed, and explained, "Our hall contains the Casavant Frères pipe organ, the largest in Canada."

Farther down the hotel on the way to the elevators was a huge telephone switchboard. "We employ 35 operators and the switchboard is 66 feet long."

"Oh, my!" My fingers touched my parted lips.

We entered the crowded elevator. The concierge turned to the operator. "Top floor, please."

The man pushed the highest button.

As we got out, Mr. Fairclough bragged, "This entire floor is reserved for King George and his royal party when they visit Toronto."

"Gosh!" I breathed out.

"Allow me to show you one of the suites."

"Oh, I couldn't impose."

"Don't worry, no one is here this week."

"Thank you. I feel very privileged." I straightened my hat and fluffed my hair.

We stood in the entryway looking at the spacious sitting room with chateau ceilings, and a full-sized radio in the corner. The dining room could seat eight people on the velvet, paisley-patterned, long-backed chairs. I followed Mr. Fairclough as he opened the French doors to one of the bedrooms, where a polished brass bed glimmered in the streaming sunlight. It was the size of three beds put together, making me blurt out, "Ooóo!" There were delicate lace pillows placed at the headboard. Off to the side was a spacious sitting room with small, elegant, carved wooden chairs. The suite was more like a miniature house than a hotel room.

The concierge stroked my arm.

I moved away. "I'd better see if my message has come."

"Of course, milady," he said with an actor's voice as we went out into the hall.

"Thank you for showing me this grand hotel."

"My pleasure. You'll have to come back again when you have more time." He gave me a flirtatious wink.

After getting off the elevator, Mr. Fairclough went to the front desk, inquiring, "Jacobs, has a message been delivered for Miss Dwyer?"

Mr. Jacobs shuffled through papers and found an envelope. "Here you are, Miss."

I reached out for the envelope and slipped it into my purse, careful not to read it in public. "Thank you again, Mr. Fairclough, it was very kind of you to give me a tour of the hotel. I thoroughly enjoyed it."

"My pleasure. Here's your suitcase. Please stop back on your way home."

I smiled shyly, grabbed it, and rushed out of the posh lobby, anxious to read the message in private.

Behind one of the tallest bushes I opened the envelope. In the middle of the plain white piece of paper was a license number: M777. I began to perspire and questioned what I was doing there. The birds chirped above me, calming my nerves a little bit while I walked toward the main street. I searched around for the vehicle, looked up and down the busy avenue, and decided to cross. On the corner was an old, beat-up Army station wagon. I glanced down at the paper and saw that the license plate number matched the number on the car.

Here goes, I thought.

I went up to the driver. He glanced at me, grabbed the paper, and handed it back. "Get in."

I threw my bag inside, sat next to it, and had barely closed the door before we sped off. My heart beat almost as fast as the engine. The journey was a frantic ride because the driver continually exceeded the speed limit. We traveled east on Old King's Highway #2.

"How far are we going?" I inquired.

The Army man glanced in his rearview mirror and shook his head.

Five minutes later, I tried to have a conversation again. "Are we almost there? By the way, my name is Mrs. Dwyer."

This time he shouted back at me, "Look, Miss, stop your yammerin'! You better learn right now to only speak when you're spoken to."

This rude comment left me feeling stupid and insecure. Why hadn't I stayed at home? At least I would have felt safe there.

The driver kept looking in his rearview mirror to see if we were being followed. I felt like I was in some strange suspense movie. There I was, in a military car with a stranger who wore an Army uniform. This secretarial job had to be for the Army, and it might be top secret.

Toronto was quite a big city, and I was surprised when we stopped 20 minutes later in such an ordinary, sleepy little town. We passed a shabby, handcrafted, country-looking sign that read: *OSHAWA.*

I willed my heart to maintain a steady beat. The driver stopped at the top of a road, got out of the car, walked around it, kicked the tires, then jumped back in. This strange act caused my heart to race again.

A four-foot-high, barbed wire fence appeared at every turn to keep the cattle inside a rancher's property. We barreled down the country gravel road in the middle of nowhere.

A lake came into view. I saw a low, wooden sign nailed to a weathered fencepost that read:

Prohibited Area
Department of National Defense

The odd clues began to add up. I suspected this was not going to be an ordinary secretarial position. We screeched to a stop at a guardhouse in front of a gate.

The guard leaned on the Army car. "Who do we have here, Bill One?"

"We got another potential."

The guard opened my car door and looked at my paper with the license number on it. "You may proceed, you're clear."

I was feeling foolish for my decision to pursue this peculiar job. If it hadn't been for their Army uniforms, I would have thought I was being kidnapped. What kind of name was Bill One, anyway? This was all beginning to feel too mysterious for my comfort level.

We passed numerous tall antenna wires protruding from the field. The lake filled my view again. *It must be Lake Ontario,* I thought. It soothed me a bit to be on the Canadian side of this Great Lake. Many times I had taken strolls along its shores on the New York side, and had always wondered what it would look like from Canada. It may be the smallest of the Great Lakes, but it looked immense to me. Dad had said it was over 190 miles across the lake to the Canadian side. It was a short, delightful drive to the lake from Rochester. I had sweet memories of Dad teaching my brother and me how to fish, and we caught many a bass or trout. When we got home, Mom would prepare our fish with her fancy, French style of cooking. So delicious!

We slowed down as we passed through dense stands of tall chestnut trees lining both sides of the road. An ordinary, but old-looking farmhouse came into view with a variety of buildings scattered about nearby in an open field.

The driver got out, opened the back door, took out my bag, and handed it to me after I stepped out of the car. He signaled for me to follow him up the creaky wooden steps to the farmhouse. We passed through a wonderful, decorated parlor, then a cozy living room with a fireplace and piano.

Chapter 8
Camp X

As we entered a room off to the side, Bill One called to a large officer behind a desk, "Here she is, Bill Two."

Did I hear that right? Bill Two? Strange names. I gripped my bag tighter.

"How was your trip, Mrs. Dwyer? Please have a seat."

"Fine, thank you," I lied, folding and unfolding my hands in my lap.

The formalities ended and he began to bombard me with questions. "What makes you think you are sophisticated enough to cope with unusual situations?" The officer held his pen above the paper, waiting to write my answer down.

"Mr., uh…I don't know your proper name. What unusual situations would a secretary have to encounter here?"

"Mrs. Dwyer, I will ask all the questions, and I need your answers. If you are accepted for the position, then you will be briefed about your training. You may call me Bill Two. We go by first names here. Please answer the previous question." His pen pointed with impatience at me.

"Well, you can see by my application that I am more than qualified to be an efficient secretary, and my typing scores exceed the average." I pushed my chest out with confidence.

The officer scribbled on the papers. "Would you be interested in going to France to work undercover for the British government?"

"Oh! Now I get it. By undercover you mean spy, don't you?"

"Kathleen." He glanced down at my papers. "I am conducting this interview and I will not be answering any of your questions."

With caution I answered, "Maybe."

The officer continued to probe, and his interrogation became peculiar. "How do you feel about the war?" Bill Two stared, his eyes piercing into mine.

"I'm a patriotic woman. My father was in the Army, and my husband and brother are presently serving our country. I'd do anything to help defeat the Nazis."

"Would you be willing to jump out of a plane behind enemy lines if you knew in advance that, if caught, you'd be tortured to death?"

"Uhhhhh," involuntarily came out of my mouth. I swallowed hard. "I have flown in an airplane once, and did enjoy it, but jumping out of a plane is an entirely different matter. It's something I can't even imagine. I do support our country, like I said, and I believe with a strong conviction that all Allied nations should work together to win this dreadful war." I fiddled with the buttons on my blouse, then stared straight into his beady eyes.

Bill Two began to shift his questions back to ordinary inquiries about my previous jobs and linguistic abilities. "All right then, Kathleen." He looked down at my papers and held his finger at one spot. "Kathleen, hummmm, you will now be known with a new code name. Kitty."

I smiled. "Kitty is what my Dad used to call me. When you say code name, it makes me wonder, what is this job really about?"

Bill Two ignored me. "You have successfully passed the final interview. We are interested in training you to become a secret agent. I must warn you that the classes are vigorous and we do not discriminate between men and women. Women are required to pass the same written and physical tests as men." He stared at me hard. "There are now a variety of psychological and practical tests over a four-day period that you must pass. An examining team, consisting of six military testing staff, including two psychiatrists, will review everything. If the team approves you, you may begin your training at Camp X. Are you interested in participating in the four-week training program?"

My blood raced throughout my whole body. "I guess so." I cracked my knuckles.

"That is not the answer I was looking for, but we'll see how you do. One more thing, Kitty, you may not tell anyone about Camp X, your training here, or write in a diary at any time. All letters will be examined before being mailed out. Do not disclose any of this information, even to your husband or family. We will give you a cover story that allows for your absence."

"Oh," tumbled out of my mouth.

The officer called out the door, "Please escort Kitty to her room."

Bill One came in, picked up my suitcase, and pushed it into my hand. I followed him out of the farmhouse. We walked through a field where there were three new buildings. He proceeded to give me a tour.

"This first building is the lecture hall. Class begins at 0800 hours sharp. Lunch, 1245; tea, 1630; and supper, 1800 hours. The mess hall is over there." He nodded toward the next building. "The farthest building is for officers only. Your housing is this way, for agents-in-training."

I held my breath after hearing the phrase "agents-in-training."

Bill One opened a door. I followed him down a long, narrow hallway. He pointed to a room marked 207. "This room's yours." He left in a hurry.

Once alone in the small room, I let my guard down and noticed that my hands were trembling. Had I made the right decision? The name "Camp X" gave me the jitters. I reasoned with myself, thinking I still could get out of this by failing the tests on purpose. On the other hand, maybe this was what I needed to fulfill my empty life and serve my country, like my family was doing. My secretarial job at the factory never helped me reach my potential after graduating from the Sorbonne, and I did enjoy a challenge.

One big, new dresser, a desk with two chairs, and a bunk bed were the only furniture in the room. It was very neat, but I could tell by the sweater draped on one of the chairs that there must be someone else I was sharing the room with. Right in the middle of one of the walls was an oversized, full-length mirror that extended from ceiling to floor. I looked at my reflection and fingered my curls under my hat, then went over to the roll-top desk. Inside there was a neat stack of paper and a container of pens and pencils. I bent down and peered under the military-style bunk beds, where I found a suitcase. I couldn't bring myself to be nosy enough to open it, and decided to look in the closet instead. On the hangers were well-pressed blouses, a few expensive-looking dresses, and two small pairs of men's pants. On one of the wooden hangers was a strange, very long wool sock, which seemed to be an odd length. As I felt the coarse material, I heard the door open.

A woman with an uneven gait came into the room. Her soft brown hair fell in waves on her shoulders. "Settling in?"

I covered up my snooping by speaking fast. "I was looking for some hangers for my clothes." I found a few, then brought them over to my suitcase.

She extended her hand. "Welcome to Camp X. Code name's Germaine." She had an unmistakable Southern accent. Germaine unbuttoned the top button of a tan Army jumpsuit that had no insignias or badges on it. She sat on one of the chairs, then stuck one leg straight out in front of her.

"K-Kitty," I stuttered, and almost forgot my code name.

"It's almost 1800 hours. I'll show you where the mess hall is." Germaine shifted her leg around.

I followed her out of the room and noticed her slight limp.

As we passed by room 250, I stopped and put a finger in one of the many bullet holes in the door.

"Don't let that bother you, honey, it was from one of the boys practicing his shooting by fooling around."

"Oh, gosh." I covered my mouth with surprise.

We sat together in the bustling dining hall. Germaine was quite at home, waving and chatting to an assortment of people lining up to get their dinner.

"I hope you can keep up with the demanding training schedule here at Camp X."

"I'll try." I looked into her sparkling green eyes. "How long have you been here?"

"A few weeks, but I'm already a trained agent."

"Why, may I ask, are you still here then?" I glanced around.

"I'm here to enhance my skills as a wireless operator. Beaulieu didn't have as good a communications program as Camp X. This camp has a topnotch wireless radio transmission program. Hydra has receiving capabilities that cost over a million dollars to build."

"Did you say Beaulieu? Did you mean Beaulieu, England?"

"Yes, it's in the New Forest, Hampshire. Have you been there?"

"No, but I've been to England a few times on semester breaks from France. I graduated from the Sorbonne University."

"Well, we have something in common. I also attended the Sorbonne. Of course, that was about 10 years ago. You must be fluent in French then."

"*Oui!* I studied Italian, also." I took a bite of a potato and noticed that Germaine held her fork in her left hand and knife in her right, bringing back memories of my college days in France.

"Wonderful. This is a good reason, Kitty, why you've been recruited."

"I suppose so."

As we finished our meal, which wasn't as bad as I thought it would be, I asked, "What's a wireless operator?"

"You'll see." Germaine got up and bussed her plate.

I followed Germaine back to our room and couldn't help noticing her limp again.

Germaine yawned and sat on the bottom bunk. I watched her untie one shoe, then pull off a long woolen sock that was identical to the odd one I had seen hanging in the closet. She removed her other shoe, then unbuttoned her jumpsuit and took it off. I stared in awe as she extended a wooden foot with a rubber sole. The prosthetic leg was held on by elastic straps that crisscrossed up her thigh, then it was belted to her waist below with a leather corset. Germaine untied the straps and pulled off the leg. The entire procedure was unsettling. I watched as Germaine put the artificial limb under the bed.

I politely glanced away when Germaine noticed. She laughed. "Don't mind Cuthbert, I couldn't do anything without my trusty Cuthbert!"

I gave a nervous giggle and went to find a nightgown in my suitcase. After putting it on, I climbed up to the top bunk. I wanted to ask her how she had lost her leg, but felt like I didn't know her well enough to broach the subject.

Germaine put her nightgown on, retrieving it from under her pillow, and told me about the hideous event of accidentally shooting her own foot off.

"I was 27 years old, working as a clerk at the American Consulate in Smyrna, Turkey. On a day off, I went hunting with two fellow workers. I was looking forward to trying out my 12-gauge shotgun from my father's collection. We had a grand picnic lunch, then hiked through a wet meadow with our guns in search of snipe in the bog. I went on ahead and came to a fence. While climbing over it, my shotgun slipped from under my arm. Its trigger caught on a fold of my hunting coat and blasted my foot. My co-workers were able to make a tourniquet with their clothes to stop the bleeding of my mangled leg. They managed to get me to the hospital. After a day, gangrene set in and the surgeon had to amputate my leg below the knee."

"What a terrible ordeal for you to go through. I can't believe you've been able to continue working." My hands clasped together above my blanket.

"I've been very fortunate. It took two weeks to construct Cuthbert, and cost over $125.00. I recovered at my family's estate in Maryland. The most difficult task was to learn how to walk and where my artificial foot was, because I had no sensation below my knee. I had to stabilize my knee with my own weight because Cuthbert weighs seven pounds."

"Oh my, I wouldn't think that it would weigh that much."

"Yes, at first I had to use crutches, then I advanced to a cane. Later, I worked very hard at walking without any aids."

"I did notice that you had a slight limp and now that I've seen your Cuthbert, I'm amazed by how well you do walk."

"Through the years, I've tried very hard to walk correctly, especially since I'm an undercover agent. I don't like to look too memorable! I've found that long peasant skirts hide my legs and do the trick when I'm on a mission."

"Tell me, Germaine, how did you become an agent?" I turned on my side, hugging my pillow.

"After I recovered from my accident I was accepted for work at the American Consulate in Venice. When the war broke out, I became a driver and joined the French ambulance service. It was a difficult job for me to use my artificial leg and foot on the clutch pedal."

"I can imagine."

"I was recruited to work for the SOE by another female agent. After completing training school at Wanborough Manor in Surrey, I graduated finishing school in Beaulieu." Germaine hesitated, then continued, "I can't say where or what I do at the present time. I'm not supposed to disclose my past to anyone, but the accident happened over 10 years ago."

"What is SOE?"

"It's the British secret intelligence service. It stands for Special Operations Executive. Camp X is part of the OSS, which means Office of Strategic Services. The OSS has offices here in Canada and the United States. The two organizations complement each other."

"I had no idea there were secret intelligence offices and camps."

Germaine chuckled. "You aren't supposed to know."

We stayed up half the night chatting away about the past. I began to drift off to sleep and dreamed that I drove an ambulance, with Fred in the back, wounded.

Chapter 9
Basic Training

I was pretty much isolated for the next four days as I took a variety of psychological and practical tests. I had no clue as to whether I was even passing them until a military officer came to my room and gave me a list of my classes.

The next morning after we had breakfast, Germaine pointed out where the main lecture hall was. "If I were you, I'd sit up close. We call the lecturer the 'Quiet Canadian' or 'Intrepid.' He may be very small, and soft-spoken, but he has immense power and is a man of action. Intrepid was a lightweight boxing champion when he was younger. Catch you later. I'm off to Hydra."

The large lecture hall was filled with many men, but dotted with several women here and there. The walls were lined with bookcases like an abundance of produce at a market stand. I scanned one of the shelves from my seat. There was an assortment of military books from World War I. I noticed many fiction books and nonfiction books about spying. I read a few of the titles as I waited for the lecture to begin. *Get Tough*, by Daniel Fairbairn; *Red Star Over China*, *Go Spy the Land*. There was even one of my favorites, *For Whom the Bell Tolls*, by Ernest Hemingway.

I strained to hear as a diminutive man said, "Welcome to Special Training School 103, or Camp X, the first paramilitary training installation in North America. My code name is Intrepid. I am the Chief of British Security Coordination, appointed by Prime Minister Churchill and U.S. President Roosevelt, who assigned me to establish Camp X."

I leaned forward to hear him better. For a man in such a powerful position, Intrepid had quite a soft voice, as Germaine had warned. I got up and moved to the front row so I wouldn't miss anything.

Intrepid continued, "Camp X has been established in Canada by the British, and was designed to help America, along with three other countries, learn the art of clandestine war. In this camp, we train Allied agents in the techniques of secret warfare for the Special Operations Executive. SOE is a branch of the British Intelligence Service with Major General Colin Gubbins as the head. The school was established on Dec. 6, 1941—ironically, one day before the bombing of Pearl Harbor—in conjunction with Major William Donovan, head of the Office of Strategic Services in the United States. President Roosevelt and his military advisors laid the groundwork for the OSS in 1939 after Poland was invaded by German troops. Camp X is one of over 60 SOE establishments. We have training schools all over the globe, including in the Middle East, North Africa, and Far East, as well as the United States. The SOE equips, trains, and helps lead Resistance groups in areas occupied by the German forces."

Intrepid turned and stretched up to pull the cord down on a large, rolled-up map from the ceiling. He retrieved a wooden pointer stick from the corner of the room. "Today I will give you the layout of the camp. It is carefully hidden here on the north shores of Lake Ontario, which is 190 miles straight across from the United States." He pointed his stick at the lake. "This way we can learn from British expertise close to American soil. The location has been chosen with a great deal of thought. We have found it to be ideal to bounce radio signals from Europe, South America, and between London and the British Security Coordination headquarters in New York. This property was a farm that used to be called Glenrath. We have kept the original farmhouse, barns, and outbuildings intact, but have added many other buildings to make this a functional training camp on 250 secluded acres." The quiet, unassuming Army officer tapped the pointer. "As you can see, we are conveniently located a few miles from the defense industries in the town of Ajax, which is the largest armaments manufacturing facility in North

America. Here, on the north side of the camp, is the Canadian National Railway line that runs parallel to the lake. Oshawa Airport is where the Royal Canadian Air Force Commonwealth Air Training School is located, five miles away. Right here is a well-guarded German prisoner of war camp in the town of Bowmanville, 30 miles away. Southward toward the lake is Hydra, where you will be required to train in basic radio transmitting techniques, including recognition and interception. Hydra has the most sophisticated equipment available."

Intrepid continued to bounce the pointer on the map. "Almost every inch of this property is being used. The roads are patrolled 24 hours a day, but to the outside world the camp appears inconspicuous. We specialize in training you for surveillance, sabotage, and covert warfare."

I glanced at a sign posted on the wall: *Know Yourself…Know Your Weapon…Know Your Enemy.* I had seen that poster before, at my interview in New York City. This time it gave me a patriotic feeling about my country.

"Are there any questions so far?" His bright blue eyes widened.

A handsome, muscular man in the front row asked, "When will we get uniforms?"

"You will be issued battle dress or casual military uniforms after this class. They will have no identifying insignias on them and must be worn during all work periods." Intrepid scanned the classroom.

No other questions were asked, so he continued, "We have thus far trained over 100 agents in this paramilitary school and expect to exceed this number by 500. There are more than 52 different courses established, ranging in duration from one to four weeks. Our syllabus covers physical training, weapons handling, unarmed combat, elementary demolitions, map reading, field craft, and basic signaling. We have some of the world's most gifted and talented officers in their trade to help train you. Lectures are combined with practical exercises." Intrepid paused and took a sip of water. "The day is divided into a number of periods and there are 30 courses to complete. The first half of the day is devoted to physical training; the second half, lectures."

The commanding officer continued. "Training is very rigorous and is run nonstop, around the clock, all year long. We will use this training to determine whether you have the stamina to endure physical, mental, and psychological stress. If you complete and pass all the courses, you will be evaluated as to what area you excel in, such as demolition, wireless telegraph work, or parachuting into enemy territory. Your stay here will be up to four weeks, with 10 weeks maximum. The physical training is extremely strenuous, and we will weed out those lacking the stomach and stamina for aggressive action. The training at Camp X is merely an introduction. Those who pass will be sent to Beaulieu, the finishing school, to enhance your expertise. If you complete finishing school, the SOE will appoint you with a personalized mission, but you will have the final opportunity to decline. Many potential agents have. Some of you will be trained to go behind enemy lines and some of you may remain in Allied territory, depending on your abilities. We are churning out an assembly line of agents, and only 50 percent of you will go on to missions. Be advised you are all volunteers, and I cannot stress enough that the training courses are very difficult. You may quit or you can be dismissed from Camp X or Beaulieu at any time. Our military staff is chosen for their skills, and they are experts in their fields. If you want to be an agent and end this war, follow their instructions with precision. We expect a one percent casualty rate, just from taking the classes. You can be culled out at any time if you do not meet the rigid qualifications. At Camp X, we will train you the best we can. There will be a salary during your training and a raise if you are accepted into finishing school."

Intrepid raised his voice for the first time. "Britain has worked hard to develop a training curriculum designed to produce spies, saboteurs, and guerrillas to coordinate all action by way of subversion and sabotage against the enemy overseas. You will be a cog in a very large machine whose smooth functioning depends on each separate cog carrying out its part efficiently. It is the objective of Camp X to clarify the part you will play and ensure quality performance. None of these important tasks will be successful unless you are all properly trained and equipped. You must learn every kind of measure for your own safety—the importance of having the right story to tell, the right kind of job to do, and how to lead your life best in accordance with those facts."

Intrepid paused, took a sip of water, then seemed to stare at each individual face in the lecture hall before continuing. "Remember, we cannot guarantee your safety. Some agents, when they get out into the field, relax their precautions and are caught. We are looking for strength in ordinary people, but never relax your precautions. The best agents are never caught. We will be watching you at all times. Do not forget that you are a volunteer and can withdraw at anytime."

Intrepid stopped his lecture when he heard a yawn. His face reddened and his voice boomed for the first time. "Keep in mind that the SOE doesn't care what happens to you. God and the empire are all that matter!"

A few frightened, shuddering noises were heard from the audience.

"We have had four years of Nazi occupation and now need help from America to destroy this fascism once and for all. We are determined that there shall be war no more!"

Everyone clapped with enthusiasm after this statement.

Intrepid took another sip of water and placed a pile of papers for each row to hand out behind them. "Before beginning class you must sign the Official Secrets Act."

Official Secrets Act

I will not tell anyone, including wives, husbands or relatives what I am doing or where Camp X is located.

I will keep my past information a secret.

I will not keep a diary or any notes of any kind at any time.

I duly swear to this oath of secrecy.

At the end there was a place for my signature and code name. I glanced around and proceeded to place a shaky signature on the form.

Intrepid collected all the papers. "I consider Camp X to be the clenched fist that will provide the knockout blow to the Axis powers."

There proceeded to be a smattering of random claps after that statement.

"Hand in outgoing mail at the Administration Office. You will all receive your own personal Army post office address, which can be used anywhere in the world. Telephone calls from the camp may be made outside working hours, but no incoming calls are permitted. Class, there will be a mandatory party on Thursday night. Everyone should now proceed to building C, room seven, to receive your uniforms, then go to your first class at Hydra. Dismissed."

He turned and proceeded to erase the chalkboard.

After getting my uniform, I went to my room and put on the drab tan jumpsuit. It was the first time in my life that I had worn pants. It gave me a sense of freedom to not have to worry about proper sitting or pulling at the hemline of my skirt. I took off my wedding band and diamond ring and put them in the pocket of my suitcase as I was told to do. I felt the indentation from the rings on my finger, which made me long for my husband.

Chapter 10
Pretty Odd Fish

Hydra, my first class, was easy to find with its three sets of massive, diamond-shaped antennae protruding high above the white birch trees. Upon entering the classroom, I sat in the front row in case the instructor was hard to hear, as Intrepid had been.

The major began the lecture with a booming foreign voice, almost blasting me from my seat. "My code name's Paddy. Call me Major Paddy. I am from Northern Ireland and a member of the Royal Corps of Signals, where I was a principal wireless instructor and taught ciphers. I helped erect Hydra, the radio station you are now in. My primary function at Camp X is to train *yous* in becoming as proficient as possible in the use of wireless transmitting radios by learning Morse code."

When the major paused, a rupture of whispering went throughout the cluttered radio room. "What did he say?" was the buzz asked by all.

Major Paddy exploded. "*Ach!* When I speak I expect *yous* to listen. *Yous* are here to learn, NOT to talk."

A lieutenant in the front row raised his hand with caution. "Major, I am familiar with the Northern Ireland accent and I'd be glad to interpret for you."

Major Paddy blew up again. "I may have an accent different than everyone else's, but damn it all to hell, I am speaking English!"

"Ah, right-o, Major, but if you wish, I could summarize all the pertinent information you need to dispel to this basic audience. Sir, your knowledge in wireless communication is so advanced it would help these common people to understand it if I recapitulated."

Major Paddy's face turned almost as red as his thick, bushy hair, and he breathed through his nostrils. "Very well. It is a complicated subject. I will give *yous* a nod when I need *yous* to summarize. *Eejits*," he mumbled under his hard breathing.

I glanced around and noticed everyone was relieved to have an interpreter.

"*Yous* will be learning a new communications system at Hydra, which was built two years ago. I'm sure *yous* seen the three sets of rhombic antennae that are strung between four telephone poles stretching from Thorton Road to Corbett Creek. This rhombic design helps the ability to cover the greatest number of frequencies in the least amount of space. The topography of the land and the lake here make it an excellent site, so that signals will arrive rapidly from the United Kingdom." Major Paddy gave the lieutenant a nod.

The lieutenant stood up, summarized, and sat down.

Major Paddy continued. "Hydra Network is a secure wartime, top-secret transcontinental wireless telecommunications complex. The intelligence traffic flows between Canada, Britain, and the USA. Messages can be picked up by signal intelligence operators listening to enemy transmissions, and then are analyzed. Our job is to convert these messages in Morse code for the UK. The advantage of Morse code for transmitting over radio waves is that it is able to be received over poor signal conditions that would make voice communications impossible. Radio messages are best if they are sped up and transmitted in short bursts that are less likely to be detected. These burst transmissions are a good technique to lessen a radio's transmitting time, decreasing the likelihood of it being located by the enemy. It is also easier to encrypt Morse code messages than to scramble voice messages."

The lieutenant rose before the major could continue and translated once again.

"When Morse code is passed in the Far East, it can then be relayed on British channels via Ceylon to London, and London to Hydra for transmission by BSC for Canadian and American authorities for analysis. Hydra transmits some of the most sensitive intelligence material to pass between secret services on both sides of the Atlantic."

Major Paddy fixed his tie while the lieutenant reiterated. He continued, "We are very proud of Hydra because it is the linchpin of British secret radio communications in North America. The creation of this clandestine transatlantic communications network facilitates American-British cooperation and is needed to win this war. With secret methods of communicating with their controllers with clandestine communications, we are able to provide a safe and reliable form of contact between spy and spymaster."

The major forgot to nod to the lieutenant, who once again got up anyway to interpret. Major Paddy began shouting something in his difficult Irish accent, pounded his fist upon the lectern, and stormed out.

"Fortunately, class, we will not have to endure further lectures on this subject. The classes from now on will be hands-on, with one-on-one instruction in learning the Morse code. Your next instruction will be on weapons and will follow this class," the lieutenant concluded.

There was quite a bit of chatter during the break. Several people got up and stretched. I looked around and noticed the handful of women who were in the class were now gone. Where had they gone? I had a feeling the word 'weapons' had chased them off.

In walked an older man who commanded immediate order. "Quiet down. We have a lot to cover. I will be teaching the weapons training class. My code name is Fearless. You may call me Major Fearless. I was chief instructor at the Shanghai Municipal Police for 33 years and was in the Royal Marines Light Infantry. I have developed numerous firearms training courses and am founder of the basic principles of combat pistol-craft and close-combat techniques. You might be taking my Silent Killing course at the finishing school in Beaulieu, if you are competent enough to pass the training here at Camp X."

I thought I saw the major glance my way, flashing me a look of doubt. I squirmed in my seat.

"I have originated innovative pistol-shooting techniques, which I shall instruct you in. There will be a brief lecture every day, then we will move outdoors for hands-on training. In case of inclement weather, we have an indoor firing range in the southwest building. I have published many books, all of which are available for you to take out of our library here."

He passed around the list of books, all with fascinating titles: *Defendu, Scientific Self-Defense, Get Tough, Shooting to Live with the One-Hand Gun, All-In Fighting*, and *Self-Defense for Women and Girls*.

I stared at the major. He looked too old to be a physical fitness teacher; his black-rimmed glasses gave him more of a studious look.

"I will be teaching you how to make good, fast, plain shots. Forget all you already think you know about weapons. We will not be wasting time on the fancy or trick shooting that most of you may have done in your own backyard or in competitions. We will be using semi-automatics that use bullets inserted into clips or magazines, not single-action revolvers that only shoot one bullet at a time by pulling the hammer back."

I turned my eyes down to the list after watching all the men poking each other and laughing with excitement. My father had been an executive for the Kodak Company and our family had never owned a gun. Most of Major Fearless's words were simple enough, but I didn't know what they meant. I had no clue what the difference between a pistol, revolver, automatic or semi-automatic was. They were all the same frightening word to me: *gun*. The men in the class seemed to know what the instructor was lecturing about. I sat upright and faked it, thinking I could go to the library after dinner.

Next, Major Fearless handed out a labeled diagram of a gun. "I expect you all to know the proper names of the parts of a weapon in order to understand my future lectures."

I studied it while most of the men tucked it under the first handout.

Major Fearless demonstrated the right way to clean a handgun. He had an assortment of articles laid out on the large desk in front of the classroom. "It's best, if you are able, to clean your weapon after every use. Failure to properly care for the weapon after firing can damage the metal of the weapon and provide poor performance in the future." Major Fearless performed the cleaning ritual.

I heard one of the men yawn.

"Rub gently to remove any signs of wear from loading the shells. Set this aside. Now, reassemble the weapon, taking special care to look over any piece for excessive wear. Once you've reassembled, wipe it down with the lightly oiled cloth and place in storage. Remember, never store a loaded weapon."

During the entire cleaning lecture, I examined the gun diagram, trying to follow all the new words.

Major Fearless continued, "I will be teaching the use of the .45 Colt and the .22 High Standard. These weapons are not simple revolvers, but semi-automatics. Tomorrow, we will learn how to use two machine carbines: the Thompson and Sten."

Most of the men cheered until the major silenced them and announced, "Class dismissed."

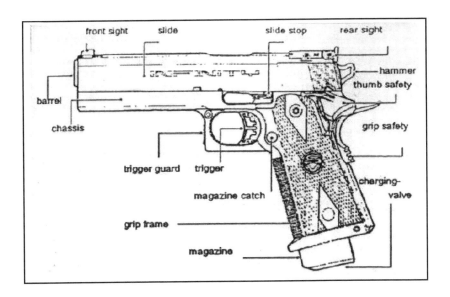

Chapter 11
Guns

The following day, after spending the night memorizing the gun diagram, I went to the weapons class with confidence.

"We will now proceed out to the far north field," the major commanded.

All of us trudged through a field full of gopher holes. My ankle bent, and I straightened it hastily out of the hole, then followed everyone with more care.

Up ahead, Major Fearless and another student carried two large wooden boxes full of guns.

"First, we will practice without live ammunition. Everyone take a .45 Colt. It is very important, class, that the first thing you do when you handle a weapon is to proof it. Take your Colt and prove to yourself that it is not loaded. This is done by first removing the magazine. The magazine release is on the left side of the grip, behind the trigger. Use the thumb of your left hand, press the catch to the rear, then withdraw the magazine. Next, grasp the slide with the fingers of your left hand, keep your elbows close to your body, work the slide back and forth two or even three times by punching it forward with your right hand. Now you know if there are any bullets in the pistol and if it's safe." He demonstrated every move, then said, "Everyone proof your Colt several times."

All the men did this with ease, as they most likely had done many times before. I held my .45 Colt with my smooth, slender hands. It was heavier than it appeared to be. Most of the men seemed to have thick hands and wide wrists. I always needed help to open a jar of pickles, my hands were so small. Germaine was lucky to have had hunting experience; this class had probably been a snap for her. The slide was awkward and hard for me to pull back with my left hand, and I could not work the slide backward or forward in order to do the proper proofing. My hand seemed to have a mind of its own and the gun shook out of control in my grasp. All the men heard me grunt when I tried to pull the slide back. They snickered; my face flushed. A good-looking, tall, broad-shouldered man sidled up behind me as tight as a baseball in a glove. He helped me grasp the slide to pull it back and forth, then stepped aside. I gave him a smile and with all my might pulled the slide backward, then forward.

"Now you've got it!" His eyes shone and he grinned.

Two other men helped the only other gals in the class, who fumbled like I did.

The gun still felt awkward and heavy in my hand. "Are there any smaller guns, Major?" I glanced back at the girls.

He responded, "Do not call it a gun. Always remember, it is a weapon. The .22 High Standard is lighter. We'll practice using it later on."

I felt intimidated and decided to not ask any further questions. I was the only one who asked questions; everyone else seemed to have handled a weapon before, except the women. I looked at them. They shyly hung out in the back of the field whispering to each other.

"Men...I mean, everyone—practice proofing your .45 for a while so you'll be able to do it fast when you're sent out on assignment. Practice, practice, practice," Major Fearless commanded.

I tried again to proof the Colt.

Suddenly, one of the men yelled, "Hey! Watch it!" He shielded his face.

The major grabbed my weapon and pointed it down. "Never point a weapon at anyone except an enemy!"

"B-but...it doesn't even have bullets."

"Don't ever point a weapon at another person unless you mean to kill him! Loaded or unloaded!" he screamed at me.

A blush crept across my face. I pointed the Colt at the ground and sheepishly tried to slide it once more.

Major Fearless announced to the class, "Whenever you handle a weapon, at all times make sure the barrel is pointed downrange, loaded or not. This is safety rule number one, and don't any of you ever forget it." His narrow brown eyes stuck to mine. "These pistols have a short barrel and a short shot range of not more than 12-15 yards. When you are that close to the enemy, you must be able to kill from any position and in any light, including complete darkness. Hold your weapon with a strong grip, as if you are trying to crush its handle. Grasp it until the tightness of your grip causes a tremor in your hand, then you ease up to the point where the tremor disappears. The natural tendency is to squeeze tighter when the shot is fired, and this makes your grip inconsistent through the firing cycle. What you need is accuracy. Your grip should not change at any time while aiming and firing the shot. Remember, crush it!" the major instructed. "The trigger finger is always kept inside the trigger guard with the fingernail resting against the front of the guard. The finger is never outside the trigger guard or it reduces your speed in fast action. Slowly squeeze the trigger; jerking the trigger will throw off your aim. Take a breath, exhale half of it, then squeeze. Once you begin pulling the trigger, keep pulling it at a constant rate until the weapon goes off. Be forewarned that the shot might startle you. Practice, practice, practice!"

Most of the men rolled their eyes. I, on the other hand, was concentrating on every word the major said.

"Now remember, class, there is never time to use the sights of the pistol when you are an agent behind enemy lines. Use instinctive pointing; look directly at the enemy's stomach, aim for this center mass. The barrel of your weapon is an extension of your arm; the pistol becomes your pointed finger. Always shoot your enemy in the belly. He won't bother you much after that." Fearless gave a dark laugh that no one else joined in on.

"You can stand as far as three feet away. But don't worry, the bullet doesn't mind traveling that far. Gut shots most of the time are fatal, because it is the easiest part of the body to hit with its vital organs. Do not ever look down at your finger and shoot from your waist, not at eye level. Stand in the proper firing stance by making sure your feet are a shoulder-width apart, with the foot opposite your dominant hand about a step past the other foot. Blade your body and stand with a slight lean forward. Make sure you're firmly balanced. The elbow of your dominant arm should be almost straight." The major demonstrated the proper stance. "Practice until your body movements become instinctive. Practice, practice, practice."

The men all shook their heads, tired of that word. This prompted the major to shout something new. "Survival depends upon speed!"

The class all held the Colts in the way that was demonstrated.

"We will now load the .45, then do some target practicing."

Some of the trainees yelled an assortment of exclamations.

"All right!"

"Hooray!"

"Some action, at last!"

The major glanced up, quite annoyed. "We must perfect loading the weapon before there will be any firing." He demonstrated the proper loading techniques, then shouted, "Men, get your bullets here!" The major pointed to the large box of ammunition. He glanced at the women and corrected himself. "I mean, everyone."

I got the magazine clip out by pushing the small release near the trigger. Next, I put the bullets, one by one, into the spring-loaded clip and slammed it into the bottom of my pistol. I practiced loading and unloading the magazine several times until it became a bit easier.

Major Fearless continued the lecture as a strong breeze came off the lake, sweeping along the surrounding hills, blowing strands of hair across my face. It gave me a sudden chill.

"Your weapon is now ready for firing. Speed in the handling and manipulation of a pistol is essential, with each hand having a definite job to do. I want you all to picture in your mind the circumstances under which you might have to use your pistol. A typical scenario would be a raid on an enemy-occupied house in total darkness. Crouch down, balance your body on the balls of your feet in a position from which you can move with speed in any direction." Major Fearless exhibited this stance. "Enter the house, search for the enemy. Listen instinctively, feel for any signs of danger. As soon as you see the enemy, without any hesitation, fire and kill him before he has a chance to kill you! Fire from the crouch position, never upright. Pistol shooting in close quarters should always happen in a split second. Speed in attack with accuracy demands aggression and extreme concentration. Remember, a weapon for spies is not a weapon for self-defense, but for attack. A pistol has a short barrel, therefore it is a short-range weapon. Like I said before, the normal combat range is 12-15 yards. When you are attacking close to the enemy you must be able to move with extreme speed. Be ready to kill from any position and in any sort of light, day or night."

We were all quiet, and listened intently.

"Class, I want you all to proof and load for a good half hour every day. Practice does make perfect. Everyone will be issued a .45 Colt tomorrow with papers and an assigned number. Keep track of it at all times and always bring it to class. Tomorrow we will go over the use of an automatic. I encourage you all to dummy practice in front of a mirror every night after your classes."

Ah, I thought. *That's the reason the full-length mirror is in the room.*

The major got a few straw-filled dummies out of a burlap bag and set them far apart in the mown field. "Stand less than 15 yards away. Get in the proper stance. Now, aim for the gut; two fast shots will dispose of Mr. Scarecrow permanently."

Everyone laughed.

He shot a few times, and the bullets landed bull's-eye, one after another, in the exact center of the dummy. The noise of the shots made me wince. Two of the men noticed and jabbed each other.

Major Fearless had us line up. All the men scrambled to be first. All the women were at the end. I was in front of them.

My turn was next and I tried to stand like the men did. I was frightened but eager. I fired my Colt. The loud blast startled me, and my hand wobbled. My ears wouldn't quit ringing, but I ignored it the best I could. I couldn't help flinching every time, before I even pulled the trigger. Each shot hit the dirt, flinging the shell into the air and out by my side, jolting me. It was what the major had called the "kick." I inhaled and continued firing my eight shots in a row. At last, I hit the straw-filled dummy one time, toward the very bottom of it. All the men burst out laughing until the major glared, silencing them.

Major Fearless shook his finger at me, barking, "You're not hitting the target because you're not firing from the center of your body. This makes your shots too low. Shoot as though your life depends on it. Speed in attack is crucial, and you must hit the vital parts of a man's body. Remember, from the center!"

He loomed over me, well over six feet tall, to help me with my stance. As he did, I couldn't help noticing that his arms and even the palms of his hands were covered with scars, maybe from knife wounds. I sighed, and wondered if I could perform the whole complicated procedure.

"The object in pistol training is maximum speed in attack with sufficient accuracy to hit your enemy. I will watch to see if you are pointing and elevating the right way from the center of your body. Don't forget—good, fast, plain shots." The major almost said "practice," but saw everyone's annoyed faces and appeared to think better of it.

We all took turns shooting at the straw dummies.

The major shouted, "Kill that target before it kills you! Shoot like your life depends on it!"

I couldn't hit the dummy, and when I did it was always at the bottom, not the center. The two other gals did just as poorly. My small hands and the weight of the .45 made the task difficult for me. I was relieved when we were given a .22 High Standard and my shooting began to improve. I hoped I'd be issued that one instead of the Colt.

"Class, keep practicing with your semi-automatics. Tomorrow I will be lecturing on machine carbines."

All the men shouted with an assortment of glee.

"Yippee!"

"Hooray!"

"Hot damn!"

The major raised his voice. "Class, one last piece of advice before we end. If all else fails, kick the enemy as hard as you can in the balls—I mean…testicles." He gave all the women a sideways glance.

I tried not to react to that uncomfortable remark when all the men snickered.

Chapter 12
Parachuting

After two hours of calisthenics, my last class of the day was parachute training. I was fatigued, but felt less nervous about this class than the weapons class. Heights had never bothered me, and I found airplanes fascinating.

We met outside, west of the communications building at what was called the "jump tower." The instructor, code name Mac, wore a Scottish-type uniform including a kilt. I couldn't stop staring. I had never in my life seen a man wearing a skirt. All I could think about during his lecture was if he jumped off the tower his plaid skirt would flip up, exposing his underwear—a sight I wasn't interested in seeing. I wondered if he wore that kilt in the freezing winter climate of Ontario. Mac's accent was indeed Scottish, but thank goodness he spoke in a slow clip, his red-orange, toothbrush mustache moving up and down.

"Here before you, class, we have a 90-foot wooden jump tower with a thick rope suspended from it. This tower was built as a way to practice falling and to learn to land. It will give you a sensation similar to jumping out of a plane."

I interrupted his lecture. "Where are the parachutes? Won't we be falling from that tower with a parachute?"

A few of the men chuckled.

"No, parachutes cannot be deployed unless you are at a minimum of 2,600 feet in the air. You might be jumping from that height in a plane, if you make it to finishing school. We'll be learning how to fall the right way to the ground from the jump tower in order to not break any bones."

While waiting in the long line to the jump tower, my mind wandered, thinking about the one time I had broken a bone. I was skipping to the store with my brother on an uneven sidewalk when my ankle bent. I heard a popping noise, like cracking knuckles. Down like a pancake I went, hands over my head, scraping my arms on the cement. As I lay there moaning, Harry asked, "Can you get up?"

In shock, I said, "I don't know, I'll try."

When I rose, my ankle throbbed with an intense, shooting pain. Immediately, I collapsed, weeping, "I can't, I can't."

My ankle continued to radiate a stabbing, sharp ache, and my arms were bleeding from the fall. Harry, at 13, had well-developed muscles. He picked me up and carried me several blocks home. The doctor came and declared that I had broken my ankle. It took a few months for me to be able to walk normally, and sometimes I still felt a weakness in that foot. I didn't want to experience that again, and was uninspired to climb up that high tower. A thought persisted in my mind that Intrepid did tell us this was a volunteer program and we could quit at any time.

"The Parachute Landing Fall, or PLF, is done the proper way by bending your lower legs with your knees held together to the side, thus so." Mac demonstrated the stance in his plaid skirt. This caused some chuckling, which he ignored. "Everyone copy me and perform this exercise on the ground."

We all mimicked the position.

Mac yelled, "PLF, PLF! You must learn this skill in order to safely transition from falling to landing in order to absorb the downward force. By using this method, it will transfer the energy of the fall to the lower legs and knees, and up the side, preventing pain and injury."

After we practiced the PLF for a long 10 minutes, he commanded, "Line up!"

We all got in line and I ended up toward the back, delaying the inevitable. I craned my neck and watched several men swing from the tower. Some yelled out a "whoopee!" while others were silent and red-faced. One woman screamed, "Ohhhhh!" the entire way down.

While standing in line, a petite blond woman chatted nervously with me.

"Too bad we don't have real practice parachute towers like my husband in Fort Bennington uses."

"What are those towers like?"

"My husband wrote and told me that they're like the '39 World's Fair towers, erected by the same company for the Army. I was worried about my husband jumping until he explained how it worked. He said that a cable pulls the paratrooper beneath the parachute to the 250-foot tower, then an automatic release drops the man to float gently to the ground. The paratrooper's chute is attached to a large metal circle suspended from a cable from the top of the tower. Vertical guy wires prevent swaying and a metal ring keeps the chute open at all times. Shock-absorbers eliminate the impact of the landing."

"Parachutes sound like a lot more fun than this tower." I looked at the rope dangling back and forth high in the air.

"I agree. You know, Amelia Earhart made the first public jump on the one built for the World's Fair."

I peered up the stairs at the exceedingly tall wooden tower. No, it wasn't the height that bothered me—what bothered me was the thought of breaking a leg and not using a parachute. I stared up at the tower and shuddered, imagining a broken leg felt twice as bad as a damaged ankle. The last group on the ground kept practicing the proper way to fall. I knew if I refused to climb the jump tower I might be sent home to mope around with nothing to do except wait for the mail. I gnawed on the inside of my cheek.

My turn was next. I climbed the tower and tried to prepare myself for the exercise, thinking, *I will sail like a bluebird coming upon a fruit-laden cherry tree.* I climbed higher and higher, viewing the luscious green hills and Lake Ontario glistening in the distance. I held the scratchy, thick rope in my tiny hands, closed my eyes, and swung off out into the air. I whirled down a deep, dark, unending black hole. My breaths came in rapid wheezes. My clenched eyelids opened and I found myself flat on the ground. I opened my eyes, blinked, and looked up at the instructor.

"Did I do it right?"

"No, you fainted. Damn girls, why do they keep sending them to me?" He pointed at the tower and yelled, "Next!"

I wobbled toward the back of the line, holding my shaking hands behind me. My turn came up too fast. I climbed the tower, but upon seeing the rope I couldn't release my sweaty hands from behind my back. Then I heard the instructor yell from below, "Jump! You're holding up the line!"

The man next to me shouted, "Move out of the way and let a man do his job!"

I climbed down from the tower. The entire line had to move off the ladder to let me off. After watching a half hour more of jumping, I couldn't bring myself to go near the steps. Thankfully, no one seemed to notice, including the instructor.

Mac announced, "To continue on to week two, you must pass all jump training tests, and the physical fitness requirements. Some agents-in-training who are unable to advance may require additional schooling, or will get 'recycled' to a different class due to lack of progress or injury."

I thought the teacher glanced my way.

"Expect soreness tonight from all the repetitive falling. Dismissed!"

Chapter 13
Morse Code

U pon entering Hydra the next morning, I sat down in one of the last remaining seats in front of a Morse code transmitter. I pointed to the corner at a group of large crates labeled *Ozopure*.

"What's that?" I whispered to the woman sitting next to me.

"Oh, you missed that part. That's liquid to cool the gigantic tubes that are required to run the transmitters."

"Isn't that something..." I mumbled.

A group of military men in the back of the room came forward and chose a few of us to teach Morse code to. Everyone's eyes studied a large chart displayed in front of the classroom. I heard Major Paddy's booming foreign voice from across the room. Thank God he didn't come in my direction or I would have failed the class.

The interpreter from the previous day's wireless transmitter lecture was my teacher. The sleeve of his uniform brushed against my cheek as he cozied up behind me and showed me how to work the transmitter.

He whispered in my ear, "You smell lovely."

The word "lovely" sounded like "loverly" in his British accent, giving me a slight tingle. I felt my bare wedding ring finger, glanced at his dimpled, clean-shaven, boyish face, and grinned at him. I recalled how much attention I used to get from all the boys in college, and I did miss it.

"This is how to handle the straight key: grasp the rim of the disk, like so, put it between your thumb and middle finger, place the forefinger on top of the key disk. Keying action should come from the elbow or forearm." The lieutenant demonstrated by holding and tapping the quarter-size black disk. "Now you try it."

I placed my hand in what I thought was the proper position. The teacher touched my arm, helping me correct my wrist. A tiny thrill ran down my body.

"Remember, don't bend your wrist. Make the movement easy, like flicking a light switch up and down. The straight key is on when it is pressed, and off when it is released. Try to do one word and I will guess what it is." He put on the headphones while I looked at the Morse code chart on the wall and typed in a word.

"Very good, SOS. Three dots, three dashes, three dots. This is the most common distress signal internationally, and an essential word for you to know how to type. You know, it was first adopted by the Germans in the early 1900s, and was signed into the radio regulations for all countries to use."

I cocked my head and listened.

"The dash is three times the duration of a dot. All Morse code elements depend on dot length. Dots are short, while dashes are long. A simple way to practice your speed is to send the same five-character word over and over for one minute. If, for example, the operator wanted a character speed of 13 words per minute, he would send the five-character word 13 times in one minute. From this, they would arrive at a dot length necessary to produce 13 words per minute while meeting all the standards. Do you understand what I'm saying?" He touched my shoulder.

I nodded, beaming.

The officer continued. "Because of this, we use a method to standardize the dot length. Each dot or dash is followed by a short silence, equal to the dot duration. The letters of a word are separated by a space equal to three dots. Two words are separated by a space equal to seven dots. The dot duration is the basic unit of time measurement in code transmission. The most common letter in English is the letter E, with the shortest code, a single dot. The letter T is also used a lot. R is a short way of saying 'I understand your message.' Make sure you get that one down. Now, practice those important letters for a while, and work on your numbers. I'll come back and check on you later." He patted my hand.

International Morse Code

1. The length of a dot is one unit.
2. A dash is three units.
3. The space between parts of the same letter is one unit.
4. The space between letters is three units.
5. The space between words is seven units.

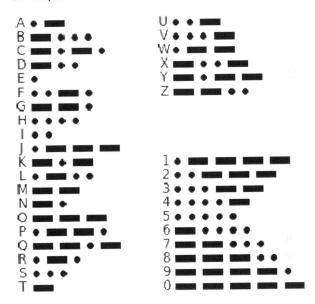

After studying the chart and rehearsing the numbers and letters, the lieutenant came back to my station. "I'll type a sentence. Tell me what you hear."

I put on the heavy earphones and tried to listen to the series of on-off clicks. "I'm not sure."

"I'll do it slower. Listen to the long and short pulses, try to tell the difference."

I blushed. "I think you typed 'you smell like a rose.'"

"You got it!"

I felt a twinge of guilt because I was enjoying his flirtation. When he moved off to the next gal, I watched to see if he flirted with her, as well.

After I practiced for a while, he returned and leaned in behind me. "Let me see you type a complete sentence."

I would type one letter and look at the chart, then another. It was cumbersome.

He took off the earphones. "I do need you to know that speed is important, because the Germans have direction finders and can pick up the signals if the transmitter takes too long. The word one chooses determines dot length. A word with more dots, like PARIS, would be sent with longer dots to fill in one minute. A word with more dashes, like CODEX, would produce a shorter dot length, so everything would fit into one minute. These are excellent words to train on to perfect your speed."

I mumbled the words "PARIS" and "CODEX."

"Listen to the tones or clicks. Once you get the hang of it, you'll find that Morse code is the simplest and most versatile method of telecommunication. Better spend a while on those words, then I'll check back with you." The handsome lieutenant paused. "What did you say your name was?"

"Kitty," I beamed.

I spent over an hour working on my speed while studying the chart and training my ear to the beeping. The heavy headphones irritated my ears. It was puzzling to me how exhausted I felt when all I was doing was sitting.

After the last of my many classes, I dragged my weary body back to my room, ready for some shut-eye. I didn't have much of an appetite and wasn't interested in dinner. My mind was still full of anxiety, wondering if I would be sent home after the fainting incident from the day before. Germaine was hard at work at the desk with her headphones on, pushing out the Morse code with a wireless transmitter contained in an ordinary-looking suitcase.

She pulled off her headphones. "How was your day?"

I hesitated and looked around before speaking.

Germaine reassured me, "Don't worry, we can speak freely in here."

"Well, to tell you the truth, I'm not sure I'm cut out to be a spy. I know that I love my country and would like to try to help defend it. My husband and my brother are both in the service. I've never been this exhausted in my entire life, but I do feel intellectually stimulated."

"Did you have trouble with one of your classes?"

"Yes, it was the jump tower one."

"Did you refuse to jump?"

"Oh, I jumped all right, but I fainted after I landed."

She searched my face with curiosity. "Hmm. How did you do in your other classes?"

"I think I'll get the hang of the weapons class, since they issued me a .22 High Standard instead of the heavy Colt."

"That's good. The camp might let you skip the parachute jump training. I didn't have to take that class because of my false leg. Make sure you spend extra time on your typing. Wireless transmitter operators are very valuable in the war effort. Why don't you avoid the jumping class, if you can't do it, and see what happens. Camp X is only basic training. You'll be evaluated before you can get into finishing school."

I sat down, took off my shoes, and rubbed my legs and feet, which were sore from jumping. "Thanks for talking this over with me, Germaine. I think I'll skip chow and get some rest and see how I feel tomorrow." I lay flat on my back, content and pleased to have a girlfriend to confide in.

Chapter 14
Machine Carbines

I awoke to a continuous metal tapping noise. Germaine was already at the desk working on her Morse code. "Good morning. You sure are up early," I said.

Germaine turned away from her desk. "It's the best way I can get my typing up to speed."

I got up and looked at the suitcase set. "That sure is small."

Germaine touched the case. "It's packed in a suitcase so it can be easily transported into enemy-occupied Europe without suspicion. The concept of concealing radios in suitcases was first developed in the '30s by the French and German intelligence services. The SOE gets suitcases from arriving European refugees. It is amazing how compact they've made it."

"How far can it pick up signals?"

"It has a range of up to 500 miles, or 800 kilometers."

"How heavy is it?" I lifted a corner.

"This is a Type A Mk III radio that was recently invented. It's smaller and 20 pounds lighter than the previous model because the radio components were reduced. This wireless is only 32 pounds."

"Thirty-two pounds sounds like a lot to carry around the country to me!"

"Don't worry. If you stick out the training here you'll become quite a strong gal."

"I know what you mean. That two hours of calisthenics every day will do that, and improve my figure."

Courtesy National World War II Museum, New Orleans, Louisiana

Germaine looked me over. "Your figure looks pretty perfect to me. By the way, tonight's a party and it's required that you attend. We'll be up late."

"I heard about it. I've never heard of a 'mandatory' party before."

"Kitty, everything you say or do at Camp X is observed, and it's important not to forget that." Germaine went back to her set.

After breakfast, I got to weapons class early. I glanced around and looked to see if more women were there this time so I didn't sound stupid if I had to ask a question. It was difficult enduring all those annoying men.

Major Fearless began the lecture. "Pistols have short barrels, and therefore are short-range weapons. Today we will be dealing with two-handed weapons with larger magazine capacities. Machine carbines are capable of full automatic fire."

Some of the men clapped. One new gal looked at me with an exasperated face.

The Major glared at the audience. "Men, uh…I mean people. Fully automatic fire is useless unless it is controlled. Machine carbines have the same principles as pistols. You must have speed in attack with sufficient accuracy to hit the vital part of a man's body. We will learn how to handle two different types of machine carbines: the Thompson and the Sten. The Thompson is an American submachine gun, invented by John T. Thompson in 1919 and averages 600 rounds per minute."

Major Fearless held up the submachine gun. A few of the men cheered, and the major again glared at them. "I expect order in my classroom. Speak only when you are spoken to. Now, as I was trying to say, the Thompson weighs 10.8 pounds or 4.9 kilograms carried empty. This makes it invaluable for close combat. It has two magazines and when fired from the hip has a distance of 12 yards. The Thompson has a tendency for the barrel to climb off target in automatic fire, which has been a big complaint against this weapon. The drum magazine has significant firepower, but can be heavy and bulky. It is also rather fragile, and cartridges tend to rattle inside it, producing unwanted noise. I will now demonstrate how to proof the Tommy. Like a pistol, it is the first thing you need to do."

The major showed us how to proof the submachine gun, then announced, "This weapon is now safe. The Thompsons used to cost the U.S. government $209 apiece. Thank God, last spring design changes brought this down to $70—much more affordable."

Major Fearless put the Thompson machine carbine down and picked up a different weapon next to it. "We have here a Sten machine carbine. This weapon was designed in '41. It fires 9mm Luger ammunition available on the continent and is a British submachine gun." The major held the gun up. "It's a fully automatic short rifle capable of firing 500 rounds per minute with a 32-round box magazine. It's very light, weighing 3.2 kilograms or seven pounds; that's three pounds lighter than the Tommy gun. The Sten can be broken up into three parts and carried in a small bag. Good for you ladies." He nodded in our direction.

After my difficulty handling a .45 Colt, seven pounds sounded heavy to me. A frown spread across my face as the major continued.

"This machine carbine is accurate up to 170 yards when fired from the shoulder. Its simple mechanism allows for stripping and can be concealed. The Sten can be fired dry and the working parts do not have to be regularly oiled. A weapon like this is handy for slogging through a swamp or crawling up a beach. Why, even fording a stream will not render the Sten gun useless as it can be immersed in water, mud, or sand and still fire. Now, let's head to the backfield to practice firing both submachine guns. Rob and John, help carry out the weapons."

As the major headed out of the lecture hall, the men chatted with excitement about trying out the new weapons. The women, as usual, were silent. We all trudged out to the field and gathered around Major Fearless. He continued his demonstration.

The major pointed to about 10 men and shouted, "Come get a Tommy gun to practice proofing."

None of the women were called, and were relieved to watch the men proof the Tommy guns before they had to do it.

"We use box-type magazines, which are good for fast, close combat. They are light, can be filled with ease, and can be carried in pockets. You can effortlessly carry up to 10 filled magazines distributed in your clothing." Major Fearless demonstrated the loading of the Sten. "We will be implementing these carbines in the daylight and at night. Rehearse until you no longer are fumbling around charging and un-charging your magazine. Always test each charged magazine in the gun to make sure that it will lock into position, or it will drop out or fail to fire."

The major watched a few of us get a machine carbine into position. He came right up to me. "Hold your Tommy gun under your arm, thus so. With your left hand grasp the fore grip, left elbow underneath the gun barrel parallel to the ground. Elbow locked under the gun—then you can turn fast on your target or enemy. Snap the barrel up, bringing your head down to the gun, but keep it under the arm. The left elbow and right arm lock the gun simultaneously. The gun is never moved independently of your body. When you depress your body it depresses your shots. Try it again!"

I struggled to perform the correct position.

"Better." The major gave me a nod.

Major Fearless shot first with one machine carbine, hitting the bull's-eye every time, then used the Sten. Everyone applauded, including the women. He pushed his glasses back toward his nose and smiled for the first time. "We'll now practice firing for half an hour with the Tommy gun, then half an hour with the Sten."

I made my way to the front, careful to avoid the gopher holes, so I could observe before my turn came up. It sure was a large weapon.

When I was next, Major Fearless commanded, "Load."

I loaded my magazine with 10 rounds, fumbling and shaking.

The major narrowed his eyes. "Ready."

I crouched.

"One."

I sucked in my breath, squinted, and fired one round.

"Ready. Two."

After I finished all the rounds, the major examined my shots on the bottom of the target and discussed firing positions with me. "The gun does not move independently of the body, and don't jump around that much. Stop firing with so much hesitation. Keep your head down. You must have speed in your attack. You are holding the weapon too loosely;

grip it, for God's sake! The body must be pressed toward the target in order for the shots to be driven deep. Think of the target as the vital parts of a man's body, and shoot without pause to take air. By next week I will expect you to hit the bull's-eye at least once. You'd better put in extra time on the range to reach that goal." His intense eyes behind his glasses penetrated mine. "Next!"

After everyone got a chance at target practice, the major announced, "In a week, class, you'd better be ready for moving and bobbing targets at varying ranges and elevations. We'll also be practicing in the dark."

One man yelled out, "All right!"

The major shot him a nasty look; most of the men had stopped their sophomoric exclamations a while ago.

"Throughout the month you will experience the most realistic, blood-curdling exercises seen outside a theatre of war, even though fatalities at the camp have been very few."

Fatalities? I thought. *Doesn't that mean death?* I questioned myself once again. *What am I doing here?* Was I even capable of all that was expected of me? My roommate was able to pass basic training and she only had one real leg. I thought about Fred and my brother Harry, then how alone I felt at home. With pinched lips, I shook my head and walked off to parachute training class with a heavy heart.

Chapter 15
A Mandatory Party

I wanted to skip the parachute class, but I didn't want to get kicked out of Camp X. I was mentally and physically exhausted from all the difficult information thrown at us in weapons class.

As I approached the tower, I reached inside myself to find the will power and courage to jump off that 90-foot tower once again.

Sergeant Mac pointed to a huge Army truck. "Class, we're jumping off a moving truck today instead of the tower. This will also give you practice at landing."

My mouth dropped open. Was I cut out for this poor-paying job? I was reluctant to follow the group toward the truck and stayed at the back of the crowd.

A gal with short, light brown hair whispered to me, "God knows what else they'll put us through."

"I know what you mean," I mumbled back.

Mac told one of the seasoned men to demonstrate the proper roll off the vehicle while it was stationary, then commanded, "Tom, show us a moving roll."

The driver pulled down the grassy field at a snail's pace.

"You'd all better pay attention, because there is only one correct way to hit the ground or it will cost you broken bones, or your life, when parachuting."

After Tom rolled off the moving vehicle, Mac instructed, "That was the way to roll to prevent some of the impact of falling. The proper way to tumble when you hit the ground is to make sure the shock of landing is distributed throughout the body, rather than absorbing all of it directly into the feet and legs."

The Army cattle truck rumbled toward us. Mac ordered the first group into the truck.

Sally, who was next to me, confided, "I'm glad Mac's not doing the roll."

I grinned. "I was wondering if he would dare in that ridiculous plaid skirt."

We practiced in the field for a while before it was our turn to load into the truck, then the instructor made us run in place while we waited. More calisthenics! The previous day's exercises had already left me quite sore. Another small group was ordered into the truck, and we watched person after person roll off the back as it drove down the field. I was sweating the whole time as I watched the spectacle. Now I thought flying off the tower seemed like more fun than flinging myself to the ground from a moving cattle truck.

Sally made an awkward tumble from the moving truck. She attempted to rise, but moaned and fell back down. It was obvious to me she had twisted her ankle. I winced after seeing her face. I looked around to see if anyone would notice, and snuck away from the group.

Germaine pulled a chic rayon party dress embroidered with white swirls on a navy blue background over her head. She got out a hand mirror and with precision applied a beautiful shade of dark red lipstick. "You're back early, aren't you?"

I felt embarrassed and tried to tell her about the truck exercise.

"I'm lucky I didn't have to take that class, either. I hope no one saw you duck out."

I lay on the bottom bunk, staring up at the top with tears pooling in my eyes.

"Are you afraid you'll wash out of camp?" Germaine continued to fuss with her dress.

"I never in my life have failed a class before," I sniffed.

"If I were you, Kitty, I'd continue to do the best you can in all your classes and skip out on the parachute training ones. The SOE accepted me and they know I can't jump."

I rose from the bunk, feeling glum. "I suppose you're right. I'm doing okay in all the other classes, but I'm worried I won't be chosen to go on a mission." I bit at a ragged fingernail.

"That's the spirit!" Germaine twirled in her fancy dress.

"You look gorgeous. Why are you all dressed up?"

"It's the mandatory party. You'd better start getting ready."

"Oh, I forgot about it. I'm afraid I didn't bring anything that fancy with me."

"Please, go ahead and look through the closet and try on any of my dresses. I have several. You're quite shorter than me, but a dress with a belt will work. See if you can find a loose-fitting one. I'm not gifted with a large bust like you."

"I couldn't impose on you for an outfit."

"I insist. By the way, this party is not an ordinary party. You'll be observed to see how you behave in a social situation while being continuously plied with liquor. The commanding officers like to watch how much you drink to see if you can hold your tongue."

"That's what's meant by a 'mandatory' party. I was wondering." I shuffled through Germaine's dresses in the closet, and found one with a belt. It was a beautifully styled, rich-looking black crepe with shearing at the shoulders and puffed short sleeves. The petite belt was suede. I got undressed and pulled it over my head. "I'm pretty lucky to have you as a roommate. I'd be quite lost here without you."

"Always remember, nothing is happenstance." Germaine brushed her luxurious, wavy hair, fashioning it up into a roll. "Wow, that dress looks wonderful on you. Smart!"

The neckline was a bit low on me, and showed off my ample cleavage. "Thanks." I pulled up the neckline as high as it could go to expose a modest amount of my bosom. I spun around in the full skirt, and looked at my reflection in the large mirror.

Germaine added the straps of her harness, making sure Cuthbert was on tight. She put on her plain brown shoes, which didn't go very well with her party dress, but she couldn't wear heels. "Are you almost ready? We can't be late."

"Let me put on a dab of lipstick and fix my hair."

"Here's one of my hats." She handed me a black felt hat that had a tall, crowned mushroom brim. The side of it displayed a fancy plaid taffeta ribbon.

"Thanks, Germaine. That adds the finishing touch to this beautiful outfit."

Germaine put on a blue velvet hat and tilted it forward. I was impressed by how fast she walked, given her condition, and followed her out the door.

The party was in the main room of the old farmhouse. All the furniture was quite new, which struck me as odd since it was wartime. The dapper piano player sang "White Cliffs of Dover." His body moved into the piano keys with emotion.

Bill One came toward me. "Hi there, Kitty." He nodded at Germaine. "How's your stay so far at Camp X?"

"Very well, thank you." I sized him up. Bill One was unrecognizable in his fashionable suit.

"What can I get you gals to drink?"

"I'll have an Old Fashioned," Germaine said.

I chimed in, "I'll have the same."

"Right-o. Good choice, coming right up."

I couldn't believe how good-looking he was in that sporty, two-button jacket with fancy notched lapels. What a splendid, rich, tailored suit. Gosh, he was dreamy. I felt a little homesick for Fred. Bill came back and handed us each a cocktail, then went to get his own drink.

Germaine snapped me out of my daydreaming and whispered, "You'd better go over to the bar and order a club soda. Drink half of your first cocktail, then add half the soda to it. This is a good way to get through the night without getting drunk, because if you're like me, getting intoxicated causes you to spill the beans, which is a bad quality for a spy." She went to the other side of the room to talk to a friend.

After she came back, we watched Intrepid with two other men. He nodded on occasion, then would say one word now and then.

"Most of us call him the Quiet Canadian." Germaine spoke in a soft voice by cupping her hand over my ear. "He's a close confidant of the British Prime Minister, Winston Churchill. Intrepid was also instrumental in making sure women were recruited into the program here at the camp."

A dizzy feeling floated over me. Around the piano, I sang with loud gusto along with the men to one of my favorite songs, "Peg O' My Heart."

Germaine put her arm through mine, pulling me back. "I think you've had too much to drink. Didn't you dilute like I told you to?" She looked at my empty glass. Several people were watching, and she said in a loud voice, "Tell me how your weapons class went."

I hiccupped. "For some reason there weren't many girls in the first class."

"I'm not surprised. Women seem to shy away from weapons, but if they don't show up they won't pass the training."

"The instructor was very informative," I replied in a formal tone, then giggled.

"Did you have Fearless for a teacher?"

"Yes, he's the one."

"Major Fearless is quite an incredible man. I had him at Beaulieu. He taught close-combat techniques, or what he calls *Silent Killing*. Here, drink my soda." Germaine pushed the glass at me and I hiccupped again. "He's famous for designing the Fairbairn-Sykes commando knife."

"A what?" I leaned into her.

"It's a razor-sharp, stiletto-style fighting dagger. I hope you'll get to practice with it if you make it to Beaulieu." Germaine searched in her purse and handed me a mirror so I could apply more lipstick.

Over in the corner was the balding Major Fearless, downing dry martinis and listening to a woman from my wireless transmitting class.

I took a big gulp of the soda. "Major Fearless looks too old to be teaching weapons training and unarmed combat."

Germaine sipped her Old Fashioned. "I heard he's over 57 years old, but he's the authority in the art of Silent Killing. Don't let his looks fool you. He's very fit for a man who trains men 30 years younger than him. He was the first white man to receive a black belt in Jiu-jitsu. Many people don't like the egotistical man, but he's the most knowledgeable on all the dirty tricks needed to survive. Why, he even designed his own fighting system called *Defendu,* and taught it to members of the police force in order to reduce officer fatalities."

"Sounds like quite a powerful man." I drank more soda this time.

"He even invented a special metal-lined bulletproof vest designed to stop high-velocity bullets and he made anti-riot equipment batons. I've found most of the instructors here are quite eccentric, but all seem to be effective teachers, and that's the bottom line for good training."

Bill One pushed his way through the party crowd. He gave me the once-over, then slurred, "So, Kitty, how do you like your classes?"

I was about to tell him when Germaine interrupted with a yawn. "I've got a lot of work to do at Hydra tomorrow. Want to turn in, Kitty?"

Bill One's face fell. "Come on, gals, the night's still young. Let's have another round of cocktails and a few songs."

Germaine yawned again. "Next time, Bill." She blew him a kiss and moved her leg toward the door.

I followed her out, attempting not to sway.

Chapter 16
A Good Friend

An annoying headache throbbed within my forehead as Germaine shook me awake the next day.

"Get up, Kitty. I know you're feeling the effects of last night's party, but it's all a test and you need to pass it. Get up!"

"Oh God, I feel awful." I stretched, then rubbed my temples again.

"Throw on your jumpsuit and let's hightail it to chow. You'll just make your first class. Here's some aspirin."

I sat up and dry swallowed the pills, praying they would work by the time I was in the wireless transmitter class. I could never cope with that instructor Paddy's Scottish accent under these circumstances.

I shoved down a bowl of oatmeal and a cup of coffee. I noticed the bustling dining room was quieter than usual. How many people were fighting a hangover like I was? Germaine and I parted ways. She headed to the lakeshore to sit under a tree and practice clandestine radio techniques of recognition and interception from her suitcase.

At the Morse code transmitting class everyone was sitting in front of their own machines. Instructor Paddy was finishing up a lecture in his difficult accent. I found the last seat available. My pounding headache began to subside.

The following week we were granted a Saturday off. I couldn't consider it a day off when it was used to hone all the new skills required to pass the training at Camp X. I decided to work on the wireless transmitter in the suitcase on the desk. Germaine came in after lunch, sat on the bunk, took her leg off, and massaged her stump. I averted my eyes back to typing, still not used to viewing an absent limb.

Germaine reached inside her jumpsuit pocket. "Here's a letter for you."

"But...no one knows I'm here."

"The camp forwards all your mail from your home."

With glee, I grasped the letter. My home address had been crossed off and the camp's address had been added.

"That's your new address."

"I'm so glad. Now I can write to my husband and brother. I've been waiting for the camp to give me my APO address."

I tore open the letter from my brother and wondered why Fred hadn't written me during the entire three weeks since I'd been there.

> *Dear Kathleen:*
>
> *I think about you often. It must be boring there in Rochester for you, all alone without Fred or Mom. Maybe you could get your old job back at Fred's factory.*
>
> *I have to share with you all about Santa Catalina, the island I am stationed on. It used to be a sparse island with sheep and livestock that outnumbered the people. Then it became a year-round vacation destination after being purchased by William Wrigley in the early 1900s. You've probably heard of him, he invented Wrigley chewing gum. Santa Catalina is one island with two coves separated by a half-mile isthmus. They call one part of the island Avalon, and the other part Two Harbors. The entire island is 76 square miles with 54 miles of coastline. It's the third largest of California's eight Channel Islands.*
>
> *Before the war, people came from all over to hunt, fish, boat, golf, play tennis, or to use it as a place to relax. There used to be motion picture actors, directors, and producers all over the island. Big bands played right here at the casino. Wrigley used to own the Chicago Cubs, and the team came*

over each year for spring training until the war broke out.

Tourist excursions were halted right after Pearl Harbor. The military took control of the steamer ships, and the Coast Guard issued identification cards to all island residents. Many of the families moved to the mainland in order to earn a living. Now, it is teeming with the military. The mild climate here makes it very conducive for a brisk swim, which I try to do every day. It has wild hills and steep cliffs with goats climbing all over. The springtime was a wonderful sight with wildflowers carpeting the grasslands. I know you would love the amazing flower called Saint Catherine's lace that towers to 10 feet high. There is an assortment of trees including wild apple, ironwood, cherry, and majestic oaks. The fishing here is sensational with marlin and tuna being caught for the servicemen to eat.

On occasion, special movie stars and big bands perform for all the troops stationed here. You would love it.

I wish you could visit me on this paradise-like island, but due to the war, it is now closed to all civilians.

Write soon,

Your brother, Harry

A tear dribbled down my cheek. With a sniff, I folded up the letter.

"What's the matter?" Germaine leaned toward me.

I closed the lid of the transmitter. "I miss my brother. He's my twin and we're very close. I'm not used to having such little contact with him."

"Is he in the service?"

"Yes, he's in the Army stationed on a beautiful island off California. I wish I could go and see him."

"You could go there on leave once your training is completed, before going on to finishing school."

"He says that they only allow military personnel. We're paramilitary and these plain jumpsuits won't pass for a uniform." I pulled at my collar.

"You could use a cover." Germaine stretched out on the creaky bunk, crossing her hands behind her head.

"A what?"

"A cover is like a story. Something you can use to tell relatives where and what you are doing during your absence. When you become a spy you'll receive a cover or disguise to conceal your real identity. You'll even be issued clothes to complete your new character. In finishing school at Beaulieu, you'll take a course in make-up and learn disguises in order to perfect your cover. I've got a great idea, Kitty. Your cover could be a WAAC."

"What's a WAAC? It sounds familiar."

"Women's Army Auxiliary Corps. If you were a WAAC, you could visit your brother at his Army base. There's a small disguise room here at Camp X, room 17. I'll put you in touch with Arthur. I bet he could fix you up with a WAAC uniform, no problem." Germaine sounded like a salesperson convincing me to buy a fur coat.

"Do you think it would work?"

"As long as you don't come out of character. It would be good for you to get some R&R after this intensive training. It gets very rigorous at Beaulieu."

"The island he's stationed on sounds so dreamy. I'd sure like to go."

"By the way, how's your speed coming along?" Germaine sat up and straightened out her good leg in front of her.

"It's okay, but I know it needs to be faster." I tapped the top of the wireless transmitter suitcase.

"Have the instructors taught you Morse code slang yet?"

"Slang? No. Tell me, what's that?"

"There are Morse code abbreviations that are universal. CQ means 'seek you' or 'I'd like to converse with anyone who can hear my signal.' OM means 'old man' or it can mean another operator or spouse or boyfriend. YL means 'young lady.' These are all typical abbreviations. Even if an operator speaks a different language, they know them. The letter R means, 'I copy you' or 'I understand your message.' The British like to camouflage their messages when beginning a transmission with DR OB, which means, 'dear old boy.'"

"That's all very handy to learn. Thanks, Germaine."

"I've got a great idea. Let's talk in Morse code. It will help advance our speed."

"Talk in Morse code?"

"Yes! Morse code is received as a high-pitched audio tone, so transmissions are easier to copy than hearing someone's voice on the telephone through the noise on congested frequencies. Morse can be read by people without a decoding device, and it can be taught as a language that's heard. The way we can talk in Morse is by saying 'dits' and 'dahs.' Dots not at the end of a word are vocalized as 'di.' Like the letter C is said as 'dah-di-dah-dit.' You try it."

I paced and mimicked Germaine. "Dah-di-dah-dit."

"See, it's simple!"

"That was fun."

"The letter Q in Morse is dah-dah-di-dah, which can be memorized by the song, 'God Save the Queen.'"

"That's neat. Dah-dah-di-dah," I copied.

"The Morse for F is di-di-dah-dit, which can be mimicked saying, 'Did she like it.'"

"This is clever. Tell me more!" I listened to all that Germaine was saying.

"Here's how the words 'Morse code' are said: Dah-dah dah-dah-dah di-dah-dit di-di-dit dit, Dah-di-dah-dit dah-dah-dah dah-di-dit dit. Rhythm is important in transmitting, like trying to speak Morse code. The opening bars of Beethoven's Fifth Symphony are played at the beginning of all the BBC broadcasts. Are you familiar with this piece?"

"Why, yes. I had piano lessons with my brother for many years at a very young age. Harry was so good at hearing the notes in their proper pitches that he would tune everyone else's pianos for a job."

"Well, the three quick G's and a long E-flat are the same timing of the notes that correspond to Morse for 'V'—di-di-di-dah—and stand for 'V for Victory.'"

I repeated the delightful, rhythmic sound.

"Once you become an experienced wireless transmitter you can identify who is sending a message."

"How can you do that?"

"You'll find that individual operators differ—for example, using longer or shorter dashes or gaps, perhaps for particular characters. This is called their 'fist' and operators can recognize specific individuals by it alone. A good operator who sends clearly and is easy to copy is said to have a 'good fist.' A 'poor fist' is a characteristic of sloppy or hard-to-copy Morse code. Every operator has their own individual style and to the trained receiver it can be detected if there is a sudden change in radio operators. Such as, if the Nazis got ahold of one of our sets and pretended to be one of us." Germaine tilted her head and looked into my eyes to see if I understood.

"Boy, Germaine, I'm learning more from you than in class. Thanks."

Germaine and I talked in Morse code for a good hour, each guessing what the other was saying.

"Kitty, you sure learn fast. I'm impressed. Your knowledge in music will help you become a valuable operator. Did you know that wireless transmitter operators in the field are called piano players, or pianists?"

"That's interesting."

I glanced at her stylish victory hairdo that she had fixed in the morning.

"Every skill you learned at home or in college may come in handy when you're an agent on a mission. I think you will become a valuable asset for the SOE."

"It means a lot to me for you to say that, because some of these classes have been quite difficult." I bit my lip.

Germaine's encouragement spurred me to study hard, using all my mental and physical ability. I'd never had a close girlfriend before, as I had been surrounded more by boys when I was in school. It was a good feeling having a confidant that I was not in competition with.

Chapter 17
A Uniform

few days later, Germaine got in touch with Arthur and he did have a WAAC uniform. I skipped breakfast and went to the disguise room.

"You must be Kitty, Germaine's roommate." He gave me the once-over and scratched his crotch.

"Glad to meet you." I curled my hair under and thrust out my chest. Harry's description of the island crept into my mind. I hoped Arthur would find me a uniform that would fit.

Arthur shuffled around the small room, which had racks and racks of various outfits, including shelf upon shelf of hats and shoes. It was a large, cluttered closet with men's and women's clothing mixed together.

"Ah-ha! Here's one!"

He handed it to me like a valuable prize. I folded the drab, tan skirt over my arm. Arthur gave me a jacket, which had a beautiful quarter-inch-wide strip of black braid on the cuffs. I felt the shiny braid, then the material of the uniform.

"It's wool. Don't you have a summer one?"

"No."

He turned away to get the other accoutrements of the uniform, which consisted of a blouse and cotton stockings. I tried on various sizes of brown shoes.

Next, he put a cap with a visor on it in my arms. "Here's your Hobby Hat. It's named after the WAAC director, Oveta Hobby. That reminds me, we better study the Women's Army Auxiliary Corps manual together in order for you to learn your cover disguise properly." He retrieved it from a file cabinet, moving so close to me I could smell an unpleasant odor emanating from him.

I stepped back. "I'm going to be late for my class. Let me borrow this for tonight." I snatched the manual from his sweaty hands, placed it on top of the uniform, gave him a slight smile and dashed out of the room.

Later that night I flipped through a few pages, but fell asleep. I dreamed about being on a ship in my smart new uniform and hat.

The last two weeks of training were grueling. On the field in weapons class, one of the trainees was killed in an instant when a bullet entered the top of his head about two inches behind his forehead, lodging in the base of his skull. Most of the men's eyes were wide with wonder, and a few of the women's eyes watered, including mine. No one discussed their feelings as we all watched Hank's body being carried off. Rumor had it that the Ontario Attorney General's office investigated the accident, and determined it was caused by a freak collision of two bullets. There wasn't even a funeral that I knew of.

When I discussed it with Germaine, she shrugged. "Death and war go hand in hand. I guess we have to get used to it."

I wasn't sure whether I could ever get used to death. The only death I had experienced was that of my parents. My loss was a deep sadness that crept into my heart from time to time, but always on holidays and birthdays. I didn't know Hank that well, but his accident made my own vulnerability sharper in my mind.

We practiced firing on moving and bobbing targets with a Sten, then with a Tommy gun. The emphasis was on realism—and live ammunition was used. The targets were constructed out of straw bales and would be set into motion by moving wires manipulated by the instructor. I learned to run through the obstacle course to try to hit sudden pop-out targets accurately with a submachine gun. One man's shots set the straw on fire and the flames spread across the field, setting the barn ablaze. Within minutes it burned to the ground. After that incident, only semi-automatic pistols were used on the moving targets. The following week a new pistol range was constructed where recruits could learn to fire as fast as possible and at short-range in the dark.

I got a moment later on to dash off a letter to my brother.

> *Dear Harry:*
>
> *I enjoyed reading your letter describing the beautiful island where you are stationed. I did get lonely waiting for Fred and you to come home, so I joined the WAACs. I am in basic training at Columbia, South Carolina. It has been quite demanding with hours of calisthenics. I am becoming quite fit! I'll be getting a leave soon and would love to visit you. Is this a possibility? Please write soon and tell me more about that lovely island. I imagine the weather must be wonderful being right on the ocean.*
>
> *Love, Sis*

Every minute of the day was now filled with crawling or running. The exercises were intense and rough. We were scaling ropes on the cliffs while bearing packs 35 feet above Lake Ontario. I enjoyed this part of training because I was not afraid of heights, though I saw that many others were.

At night we were driven to some unknown location and were given a map and compass to find our way back. I got very little sleep and was looking forward to some R&R with my brother. His return letter confirmed that I could visit because I was supposedly in the WAACs.

At last, my training at Camp X was completed, and I was granted enrollment in the finishing school at Beaulieu, England. I had a feeling that they overlooked my failure in parachute training because I excelled in wireless transmitting. I was able to obtain an extended leave in order to take the long journey out west to visit Harry on Santa Catalina.

I was teary-eyed saying goodbye to my roommate, Germaine. She had enhanced my growth to complete my basic training and I could not have done it without her. I hoped somehow I would see her again.

It was quite a task to get to California. After getting to New York City by bus, I took a coast-to-coast troop train in order to get there. I dressed in my disguise of the WAAC uniform and was given falsified papers that facilitated my venture.

We were packed into the train like weeds taking over an abandoned field. There were fixed seats facing one another, and hard, wooden seats with a bit of carpet on the top. Sailors were sprawled out in every available space. Their wool, pea coat sleeves rubbed against my cotton stockings. I pulled my Army skirt down toward the dirty, littered floor. Peanuts crunched beneath my feet. Legs touched legs and there was no escaping the smell from those whiskery men. I wished I had a window seat in order to distract myself from the squalor, but then I noticed the curtains were drawn tight even though it was daytime. An ugly, cigarette-smoking sailor tried to play "kneesy" with me until a mouse ran up the aisle in front of him. The men threw peanuts at it, hooting and hollering the entire time. I closed my eyes, hoping the nasty little thing wouldn't jump into my lap. Oh, this would be a long, stuffy, unpleasant journey.

It took five whole days to get to Texas on that train. I missed climbing the hills above the beautiful lake at Camp X. I would have preferred sleeping in the Pullman sleeper car, but the beds were placed together too tightly. The women were scarce, so I stayed put and was happy to get more room when some of the men went off to bunk. I dozed off, and dreamed about the island I was soon to visit.

I was awakened with a start when a loud poker game broke out. The cigar smoke and the uproar of cursing jerked me out of my deep sleep. The atmosphere of this wartime train was beginning to wear on me.

Chapter 18
USS Avalon

The delicious, full July sun warmed my face upon reaching Long Beach, California by bus. While standing in line at the ship terminal, with a slight amount of fear, I fingered my fake Army ID and tugged at the front of my snug uniform. I examined the card, which read WAR DEPARTMENT—an identification card from the adjutant general's office in Washington, D.C. The small photo of myself in uniform added to its authenticity.

The officer behind the desk asked for my identification, looked at it a short while, then with a casual air tossed it back to me and yelled, "Next!"

I stood in the long, snaky line, duffle bag in hand, to board the *USS Avalon*. The ship was a dull battleship gray. The clear, calm ocean bay was very inviting and I hoped I could sit or at least stand on the outside level to enjoy the view of the water.

As I moved up the ramp, an officer yelled, "ID!"

I fumbled through my Army purse and handed it to him. He glanced at it and pointed for me to get on. I followed all the people in uniforms and tossed my duffle bag onto the big pile on the bottom deck. I pushed through the crowds, and found the stairs leading to the outside. My brown heels clicked on the metal steps, and I squeezed myself through all the people so I could feel the ocean breeze. The salty air tickled my nose in a pleasant way. I held on to a railing, and the steamship's rich bass horn announced its departure in a deep baritone. The *USS Avalon* moved in slow motion out of the bay. Steel cables were moved when we entered the harbor. I wondered why they were there.

A handsome Navy officer stood quite close to me, as the ship was filled with servicemen. We were packed in as tight as an enormous collection of novels in a bookcase.

The Navy man turned to me. "Is this your first trip to Catalina?"

"Yes, I'm on leave. I'm visiting my brother, who is stationed there."

I had to contain myself from feeling his fresh uniform coat and felt like unbuttoning the large, shiny gold buttons displayed on the front. I nodded and smiled when the captain spouted fact after fact about Catalina Island, trying to impress me.

"Two Harbors is where the Coast Guard officer's quarters are located. That's where I'm headed. It used to be quite a wilderness when the Indians lived there." The officer leaned close to me.

I interrupted him. "I love your handsome Naval uniform. It's much more distinguished-looking than my brown one." I buttoned and unbuttoned my jacket, which was one size too small.

"Thanks for the compliment, but this is not a Naval uniform. I'm a Merchant Marine." He stood up taller, and with pride brushed some lint from his sleeve. "I know it looks similar, but to the knowledgeable eye there are noticeable differences."

"Oh, pardon me. I'm new to the armed services. What's the difference between the Naval uniform and the Merchant Marines uniform?" I didn't care, but knew that he did. I tilted my head, smiled, added my cap, then curled under my hair with my fingers, trying to restrain myself from touching those buttons.

The captain made me feel so tingly warm, and his deep, resonate voice spread throughout my body. I tried to focus on what he was saying. He stared at my hand and appeared to be looking for a wedding ring.

The officer looked out into the ocean while the steamship cut through the foam. "Merchant Marine uniforms are not bought off the rack, but are made by a tailor to fit the individual mariner who commissions it. The uniform is black, not navy blue. I commissioned two, one for the winter and a lighter one for the summer, since I wasn't sure where I would be stationed."

"I love the buttons."

"Because I'm an officer, I have eight brass buttons instead of the non-officers' six. Look, we have the shipping company's 'house flag' displayed on them." He turned a button out for me to look at.

I grinned and felt the fine, raised metal surface.

"The black shoulder epaulettes tell the officer's rank. See my diamond-shaped rank rings? They're made of French gold braid and are quite expensive." He touched them as though they were money.

I gave him a slight smile, but he was beginning to bore me with his self-centeredness. Islands were beginning to appear in the distance. I knew we must be close to Catalina. My heart quickened at the thought of seeing Harry. I hadn't seen him since Mom's funeral. Fond memories of our childhood filled my mind and I thought of us sitting at the piano together, playing 'Chopsticks' with joy. My fingers bounced with a rhythm on my Army skirt, until I was distracted by a silver flash.

"Gosh, look at the fish!" I pointed toward the back of the ship.

Other people were beginning to point, as well. The fish were flying behind us. Their fins were like dozens of glittering knife blades thrown into the air. They leaped in and out of the waves, spreading their wing-like fins while their iridescent colors flashed about.

"Those are California flying fish. They can glide on their outstretched fins up to a quarter mile. The fish launch themselves into the air, vibrating their tailfins in order to taxi along the surface. The flying fish use this tactic to escape predators." The captain cleared his throat.

"They're astonishing!" I watched the silver streaks as they flew behind the ship in the sea air.

"Look over there, we're approaching Two Harbors now."

"I can't believe two hours have gone by already."

The rugged cliffs were surrounded with an assortment of military craft.

"Without all this war equipment, the island would look desolate.

Before the war you'd only have seen yachts and fishing boats. It used to be a yachting destination until the war broke out. Why, a few weeks after Pearl Harbor, our coast was attacked by two Japanese submarines 100 miles from here. They torpedoed a Union Oil tanker, and the *USS Idaho*. A month after that, three more Jap subs were sighted within five miles of Catalina. The Avalon Fire Department reported that the county Fish and Game boat saw three Japanese subs about five miles offshore at Silver Canyon at two in the morning," the captain animatedly explained to me.

"I had no idea that there were so many Japanese sightings here. I thought they only attacked once during Pearl Harbor." I leaned on the ship's railing.

"Yes, the military had to take over all the steamer ships and all tourist excursions ended. Now, there are radar and lookout towers manned 24 hours a day to keep close watch on the open ocean for any signs of Japanese invasion. Did you notice the steel cables that had to be moved so the steamer could enter the Los Angeles harbor?"

"I did. I wondered what they were. "

"They were added to prevent any enemy submarine invasions." The captain straightened his hat when a sudden breeze came up.

"Captain, you're a very knowledgeable man. I've been isolated from the war at my Army base. This island makes me realize how important it is for us to defend ourselves." I touched the sleeve of his fine Merchant Marine jacket.

"Where did you say you've been stationed?"

"South Carolina." I tensed up, trying to get used to lying. I knew I had better get comfortable with my new cover, since I would be spending time with my intuitive twin brother.

We passed the *USS Cabrillo,* which was taking more troops to the island. The officer told me this steamship used to have a glossy white paint, but it had to be camouflaged gray for wartime.

As we passed Two Harbors and continued to Avalon Bay, many slippery-looking, black-headed creatures were swimming about. The captain noticed my curiosity. "Those are sea lions."

"What adorable looking puppies!"

He smiled. "Which hotel are you staying in?"

"I'm not sure."

Upon reaching Avalon Bay there were huge anti-aircraft guns pointing at us, reminding me that this vacationland was ready for an invasion at anytime.

"What's that beautiful round building?"

"That's the casino."

There was a flurry of activity when we approached the dock, and I lost contact with the Merchant Marine captain. Everyone scrambled down below to get their duffle bags. I squeezed myself through the mass of uniforms, not looking back at the captain, who yelled, "Miss!"

It took a long time to disembark over 1,000 passengers. I shuffled off the steamship onto the pier among the crowds of service personnel and stopped to linger on the ocean bay. My eye caught a bright, rich, orange-colored fish. *They sure grow huge goldfish here*, I thought. Long, fat, leathery seaweed waved from far under the surface of the water. From the steamer landing, I looked around for Harry. I swirled my hand in the water, finding it was quite tepid. The taste of it on my fingertips was a delightful, salty flavor, unlike Lake Ontario.

Chapter 19
Santa Catalina
Island

"**H**ey, Sis!"
I turned my head toward the familiar voice, searching through the crowds of military personnel. There was Harry, in a dapper Army uniform.

He looked me over, and instead of a peck on the cheek he gave me a salute. I thought fast, and awkwardly saluted back. Then I threw my arms around his tall frame, giving him a fierce, strong hug. Harry squeezed me back and gave me a kiss on the cheek.

"You made it. I've been looking forward to sharing this gem of an island with you. How was your trip?"

"The train ride across country was tiring, but I adored being on the *USS Avalon.* That was the highlight. I got to see the flying fish and sea lions. A captain, who stood next to me during the trip, was well informed about the island and told me all about it."

"Great. There's a lot to discover about this wonderland, even though the military has taken it over and it's not the playground that the storekeepers tell me it used to be. Here, let me take your bag."

I was used to being self-sufficient at Camp X, so it was nice to have him help me like the gentleman he was. "The island is as breathtaking as you wrote it was, Harry. I love the ocean with the rugged mountains, and those giant goldfish at the pier are beautiful. Is everything here that big?"

Harry chuckled. "You must mean the Garibaldi. They look like goldfish, but they're called Garibaldi and are more than twice the size of a goldfish. Wait until you see the casino."

"I saw it from the ship. It must've been quite a feat to build it in a circular design that close to the water. Is it for gambling?" My mind wandered back to the attractive captain.

"No, it's used for dancing and entertainment. The word 'casino' is Italian, meaning 'gathering place.' There's boxing there tomorrow night. I'll take you—that is, if you're up to watching a man's sport." He searched my face, waiting for a negative reaction, but got none. "The famous boxer, Jack Dempsey, sparred against a staff member in a temporary boxing ring set up on the beach last week."

My extensive combat training had numbed my distaste of male contact sports. I thought fast. "I'm anxious to see the inside of the casino. I might be able to sit through boxing." My thoughts flashed back to my training at Camp X. It had toughened me up and I knew I could handle watching the rough sport.

We walked down the crowded street, seeing uniforms from many branches of the service.

"Where are your barracks, Harry?" My eyes remained on the bay where all the service ships and boats were docked, all lightly rocking on the gentle sea in the breezy, salty-smelling air.

"Don't worry, you won't be staying in my barracks. You'll be staying at the fabulous Hotel Atwater."

We strolled past boarded-up shops. I wondered what they had looked like before the war. I could make out the word *Candy* on one shop and *Souvenirs* on another. One closed store had exquisite tiles outlining the entire corner of it. I bent down, and with a finger felt the smooth tiles, which had a light red, clay background. The glaze had distinctive colors: light green, blue, coral, turquoise, pearly white, beige, powder blue, black, and Mandarin yellow.

"Aren't these tiles stunning?" I said.

"You'll see them all over the island. The designs are used on tabletops, wall hangings, and even lamps. Wrigley—you know, the chewing gum guy I wrote to you about—he first found clay deposits in the '20s and got the Santa Catalina Island Company to invest in a tile factory. Many artists were then employed and several thousand pieces of tile a week were produced. When we go to the casino, you'll see huge murals of tile displayed on the entrance."

"Harry, I asked you before, where are your barracks?" I interrupted.

"Oh, they're not on this side of the island. They're on Two Harbors." He led me down a small side street.

"I'd love to go to Two Harbors. I saw it on the way here. It looked so mountainous and primitive."

"Here we are, this is the Hotel Atwater. They have over 160 rooms. This hotel is one of the newest. St. Catherine's and the Hermosa are full with station personnel and military families that are living here now. Most of the Marines are at St. Catherine's. It used to be quite a posh hotel until the military took over." Harry paid and checked me in. "Why don't you freshen up a bit and I'll meet you back here in an hour for dinner."

"Thanks, Harry. It's so nice to see you again and to share this beautiful place with you." I embraced him and went up the three flights of stairs to my room. The shower was down the hall, and the warm water soothed my tired body. I slipped on one of my favorite dresses. It was a navy color with small white polka dots and had a fashionable white sailor-type collar with contrasting buttons. It felt nice to get out of that tight, hot wool uniform.

My brother picked me up in the lobby. "You look a lot more comfortable now, Sis. That Army uniform seemed very snug."

"I'm glad I changed. The Army didn't have the right size to issue to me." I glanced out of the hotel entrance, ready to leave.

"Really?" Harry questioned.

"Where are we eating?"

"Right here. This hotel has a cafeteria that serves over 1,500 people. As a matter of fact, it's the largest in the world with two different street entrances and covers the entire block."

We had a wonderful dinner and I enjoyed my meal of fresh albacore. Harry told me that he'd had his fill of that fish. The government had contracted the commercial fishermen to continue fishing to provide food for the military, so there was more than enough albacore for all of Catalina Island. After dinner, we parted company so that I could rest up for the activities that Harry had planned for the next day.

I arose early so I could stroll around the colorful little town. There were swarms of Merchant Marine trainees marching up Sumner Avenue in Avalon for morning calisthenics. Farther up the hill, I watched hundreds of Maritime servicemen marching in review in their dress white uniforms on the parade grounds. It was an inspiring sight, and left me with a patriotic feeling within my heart.

Courtesy Catalina Island Museum

"Harry, over here!" I shouted, seeing my brother. I made my way back to the hotel.

"Hi, Sis. Hope you got a good night's sleep. Let's go over to the Boos Brothers Cafeteria. They have a pretty good breakfast there."

"Wonderful. Hey, what's that beautiful tower on the hill?"

"That's the Chimes Tower. The chimes have been tolling on the quarter hour since it was built in '25. Someone told me it used to be set on automatic to strike on the hour, half hour, and quarter hour until the military landed here."

"It must have been a nice, homey tone for all of the town to hear."

We walked to the corner of Metropole and Crescent Ave. and had a casual breakfast at Boos Brothers. I was the only gal there and couldn't help noticing many of the servicemen watching me.

"It's beginning to get warm out. Did you bring a bathing suit? I brought mine from the base."

"I did. I'd love to go for a swim in that lovely, calm sea water."

"Great. I'll meet you at the casino. It's right on the way to Descanso Beach."

After strolling back to the Atwater, I changed into my floral print bathing suit with the nice flared-out skirt, then put on a casual dress to cover it. On the way to the casino I passed a booth with WAR STAMPS written across the top. Two ladies were selling war bonds to a long line of military men.

Courtesy Catalina Island Museum

Many of the buildings along the way had a Spanish colonial appearance. There were fountains, and brick and tile benches with planters made with the Catalina tile. Palm and olive trees lined the way, giving the town a feeling of friendliness and leisure. All this beauty contrasted sharply with the sight of marching uniforms and guns.

The boardwalk through the wooden arches toward the casino was delightful. I ran my hand along the top of the serpentine wall and spotted one of those Garibaldi fish darting in the water on the other side of the walkway. Up ahead was the jewel of the island, the casino. It rose above Avalon and I counted it to be 12 stories high. The casino was surrounded by the sea on all three sides, its white façade gleaming in the summer sun. I reached the entrance, where Harry stood touching the tile.

"What a magical island this is, Harry. Too bad there's a war going on."

"That's for sure. An islander told me that before the war the entire casino used to be lit up at night, making the island look very romantic."

The grand front entrance was tiled in a fantasy marine life scene.

"These life-size mermaids glazed on the tiles are very surreal and sensual."

"Wait until you see the inside tonight at the boxing match."

Courtesy Alan Barlow, Fine Art Photography

We continued along the boardwalk to Descanso Beach, both of us deep in thought. Harry lay on the sand in the summer sunshine. I went and tested the water with my bare feet and decided to warm up on the shore before getting into the chilled, salty water.

"Harry, I think I've almost been all over this tiny island except for Two Harbors. Can't you take me there to see where you're stationed? After all, I'm in the Army. Aren't there any women there?"

"Sorry, Sis, it's top...I mean, it's too hard to get to and outsiders aren't allowed."

"Really? Why's that?"

"Let's take a walk out into the woods. I have at feeling we have a lot to talk about."

We were silent as we headed into a thicket. Harry led the way, and found a spot on a rock cliff for us to sit on. A fox peered out at us from the nearby brush. Crows grouped and circled in the sky, then squawked nonstop at us.

Chapter 20
Spies

"Kathleen, I've been wondering about a few things. When you got off the ship you didn't salute me the right way. I know how important this is and you should have learned this in basic training. Also, your uniform does not fit you properly. A uniform that fits like that would not be permitted in the Army. Besides, why were you wearing a winter one? Where did you get it, Kitty?"

Harry questioned me like he used to when I would lie to him, like when we were kids. It brought back a memory of when I had stolen a candy bar and he knew I didn't have the money to buy it.

"I'd like to know why you won't bring me to your base. I think you're lying to me, also," I said.

My determined eyes bore into my brother's identically shaped orbs. A bald eagle circled eight feet above our heads, then glided deep into the canyon. We were close siblings, not only from having shared a maternal womb at the same time, but because we had done almost everything together. I had been nervous that he would discover my cover, just from the instinct of being my twin. My plan had been to avoid as much discussion as possible about the Women's Army Auxiliary Corps. I never did read the manual.

"We're twins, Sis, and I think we're keeping secrets from each other. It's time to spill the beans."

In a defensive mood, I looked away beyond the cliff into the bright blue ocean. "You first."

"No, you first."

"All right, Harry, I know I can't fool you, as you can't fool me. I didn't salute you in the proper way and my uniform doesn't fit right because I'm not in the Army. Actually, I've been wondering if you're really in the Army."

"Oh, I'm in the Army all right. Where'd you get that ridiculous tight uniform? Besides, it's an officer's uniform. I knew by the black braid on the cuff. I know you are not an officer in basic training."

"I'm sworn to secrecy, but I know that's never a possibility when it comes to talking to you. I completed basic training at a military intelligence school, a secret SOE camp." Sweat beaded up on my nose, and I wiped it away with my finger. "I told you my secret, now it's your turn."

Our conversations of "your turn" and "you first" were very familiar to me.

"Well, it is obvious this could only happen to twins. I'm in an Army OSS school here on the island."

I gasped, then we both laughed at the same time.

"Hot damn, if that doesn't beat all!"

We hiked back down to the sand, stretched out on our towels and whispered secret stories, laughing with delight.

"Where are you going after SOE school?"

"I'm not done with my training yet, and have to complete finishing school in Beaulieu, England. And you?"

"I'm stationed at Gallagher's Beach in Toyon Bay, about two miles northwest of here. It's isolated and surrounded by steep mountains. No one knows it exists, including all the military personnel stationed on this island. Better keep your lips buttoned. After I become an expert at martial arts, weaponry, explosives, and the other survival techniques, I'm scheduled to ship off to Burma for behind-the-lines intelligence work."

"Where's Burma?"

"In Asia."

"They're sending you that far away?"

"Yes. I've been trained for it. The rough, isolated area at Gallagher's

Beach has been a good training ground for learning jungle combat."

"Oh, Harry, will it be dangerous in Burma?"

"There's a good possibility, from what I hear."

The weather was quite balmy for July. The gentle ocean waves were inviting. Harry got up from his towel with excitement, shouting, "Race you into the water!"

Sweet memories of my brother saying the same thing at Lake Ontario came back to me. The water here was a bit numbing at first, but then refreshing when I got used to it.

We swam far out into the sea, then floated for a while, bobbing around. I spotted a flat, fattish fish with a long, dagger-like tail.

"Oh my God, Harry, did you see that huge, fat fish?"

"It looked like a stingray. You can tell by its tail."

The glimmering sunshine played like diamonds in the vast, open sea. We splashed each other and had a gay ole time in the cool but calm water. A large bird flew overhead.

"What kind of bird is that, Harry?"

"It's a pelican. Aren't they big?"

"Yes, so is the seaweed." I threw a slimy piece that looked like a beaded necklace at my brother. We both laughed.

Harry told me tales while we had a nice private swim. "You should have seen me, Sis, with my piano fingers skinning a wild Catalina goat and a boar. We were given a knife and a fishing line for a three-day survival test. Go ahead, feel my muscles!" He swam up against me.

I pinched his arm. "I meant to tell you how buff you look now!" I went on my back, giggled, and kicked some water into my brother's face.

"This has been an ideal place for training to go to Burma, with its steep canyons and hills. All the coves and beaches provide for all kinds of field exercises. You should see all the bison in Two Harbors."

"You mean buffalo?"

"Yes, they're astounding creatures with long, shaggy coats, about six feet tall and weigh over 700 pounds. I love seeing these gentle giants at my base. They're not native to the island but in the '20s, 14 were brought in for the making of Zane Gray's movie *The Vanishing American*. They've multiplied to over a hundred now."

"I love the ocean water. It's very relaxing. Burma sure is far away. I wonder where I'll be sent on a mission?"

"Sis, I must confess, I can't believe they're using girls as spies. Does Fred know?"

"No, and I don't intend to tell him. I hope he won't be able to guess, like you did. You know, Harry, I have a right to serve my country as well as you do, and I bet I've learned as much as you have. You should see me shoot a Colt .45 and a Tommy gun. I have a damn good aim. Morse code is becoming my specialty and I'm up to 20 words per minute on the wireless transmitter." I hit the water with my hand, spraying it into the air. "This is becoming quite a nasty war. I've been hearing about the Jewish people losing their houses and their businesses, then being shipped off to work camps. Besides, there are plenty of girls in training at the spy camp."

"That's hard to believe, but with this war escalating I'm sure we need all the help we can get."

I headed back to the sandy beach, lay on my towel, and listened to the rocking, rhythmic waves. The warm, toasty sun kissed my eyelids, and I almost drifted off to sleep until I heard Harry get on his towel next to mine.

"As I was saying before you got out of the water, Catalina was a very popular place to film movies."

I stretched, enjoying the warm sun. "Like what?"

"*Mutiny on the Bounty, Treasure Island, Old Ironsides* and *The Ten Commandments* are some of the films that were shot here before the war. One of the servicemen told me this island has served as a backdrop for more than 100 motion pictures."

"Wow, Harry, I feel very fortunate to have come here for some R&R. The schedule at Camp X has been very tiring and demanding." I jerked my head around to make sure no one heard.

"I knew you'd love Catalina. I was advanced to training instructor and I train Japanese-Americans to fight for our country," Harry whispered while bragging.

"There are Japanese here?"

"At the camp we have Nisei. They're second-generation Americans of Japanese descent. Most of them were born in Hawaii or California. Most of them can't even speak Japanese and have never been to Japan. They're housed and trained in isolation at Gallagher's Beach. That's why I can't bring you there."

Courtesy Catalina Island Museum

We continued to spill our secrets, finding it very cleansing. After a while we dried off and walked up the path toward the casino. I pointed to the huge guns mounted at Casino Point.

"Those are 20mm anti-aircraft guns. The sentry posts guard the island 24 hours a day. See that airplane up there? It's an A-27 towing a target sleeve for the military to practice firing at a moving object. There have been many incidents of Japanese submarines right here in our waters. Last month, the Mayor of Avalon took his fishing boat between Santa Catalina and San Clemente islands. He had a frightening, foggy morning encounter with a Japanese submarine drifting on the surface of the water. He accelerated back and reported it to the Coast Guard Station. But don't you worry, we're well protected here."

We walked back to the hotel.

"I'll pick you up for dinner. I know a good restaurant where we can eat before we go to the tournament."

Courtesy Catalina Island Museum

Chapter 21
Vacation

That evening we had scrumptious breaded veal cutlets at John's Café on Crescent Ave. near the Boos Brothers Cafeteria.

Inside the round, opulent casino, many plush, red-velvet paisley couches filled the entire lobby. The walls had a rich, dark grain of carved walnut with a ceiling of sparkling, twinkling stars.

"Harry, this is dreamy." I sat on one of the couches and smoothed the soft fabric, bouncing on it a little.

"Come on into the theater, Sis. The match is about to begin. Besides, you can enjoy the art inside."

The Avalon Theater hosted boxing every Friday night. The boxing ring was set up on a huge stage. Harry told me volunteer recruits got rewarded with a steak dinner and a liberty pass. I found the boxing tournament obnoxious and boring, but I entertained myself by studying the large fantasy murals on the walls in the state-of-the-art movie palace. The murals reflected the secret underwater world of Catalina. The paintings on one wall had a movement of vivid colors, with fanciful sea creatures swimming among the towering kelp forest. The style of the artist was reminiscent of the frescos I had seen in Italy during college. The farthest wall on the other side of the theater had leaping horses that depicted a story of California's early history. *What an imagination this artist has,* I mused, all the while listening to punches and groans. The brilliant, colorful lights set a mood of wonder and awe.

I glanced away from the murals after one of the opponents landed many devastating blows and the bell rang, signifying the round was over.

I thought back to Intrepid, one of my instructors at Camp X, and how he had been a lightweight boxing champion. That world seemed very far away for me now.

The grunting of the boxers and the screaming obscenities from the audience were beginning to annoy me. I tried to distract myself by studying the paintings again. I spotted an organ on the side of the stage. It was immense, and seemed to have over 50 pipes that were fitted into the ceiling lofts covered by grillwork. It looked as old as the turn-of-the-century pipe organ that the concierge had shown me at the hotel in Canada months ago.

On our way home, Harry spouted with enthusiasm, "That was some fight!"

"I don't care for boxing. The defensive weapons class I had at Camp X had more of a purpose and interest for me. I did appreciate you taking me though, because I loved seeing the inside of the casino. Those murals are surreal and the pipe organ is very impressive."

"There are church services held there every Sunday, and it's used as a lecture hall for the military the rest of the week. See that yacht club? Even that fancy building has been converted into classrooms for Maritime service trainees."

It was pitch black out and I held on to Harry's arm. A marine layer of fog had crept in when the evening cooled down. "It's so dark."

"Before the war, the casino would be lit up so bright that the residents called it a sparkling gem. This island must have been the cat's meow back then. I heard there used to be glass-bottom boats for the tourists to take to see the amazing underwater world of Catalina."

"Oh, Harry, I would have loved to have gone on one of those glass-bottom boats." I looped my arm through his, which helped warm me against the chill of the night.

"Up there on the hilltop they started construction on an airport before the war." Harry pointed toward the dark cliffs of the island. "Mountaintops had to be leveled and valleys filled in to provide a flat surface for the runway. Then the war broke out, and the military was afraid that the Japanese might use it. Now, cables and utility poles are strewn all over the runway to discourage any enemy landings."

"I hope we can return after the war like plain ole tourists. I'd love for Fred to come, too. It could be a happier time for the three of us."

"Let's plan on that, Sis. We'll all celebrate the end of the war on this fantastic island."

We arrived at the Atwater.

"Tomorrow's your last night here, and thank your lucky stars there is a big band playing at the casino. Let's go for one more swim during the day, then we'll cut a rug tomorrow night."

"I haven't danced in a very long time. That would be a dream come true for me. What band is playing?"

"I'm not tellin'," Harry teased. "I want you to be surprised!"

"You know I love surprises. See you in the morning. 'Night, Harry."

I awoke early to the sound of a band playing the "St. Louis Blues March." After getting dressed, I wandered toward the joyful sound. There in front of the El Encanto Plaza was the U.S. Maritime Service Band. The trombone player gave me an unmistakable wink.

Courtesy Catalina Island Museum

118

As I stood there, hundreds of white uniforms streamed past me. I followed the swarms to the ballpark, where Harry said the Chicago Cubs used to train before the war. I watched the troops do their morning calisthenics. Some of the men took their shirts off, and with delight I watched their muscles pump up and down in the temperate climate.

After breakfast, the fog lifted early and we decided to go for a swim in Descanso Bay. Harry and I passed by row after row of wood and canvas bungalows in the center of Avalon. Harry called them the "Island Villas." They were used by many of the military trainees.

"They're so close and crowded together."

"I heard that when the island was first open to tourists in the 1800s, people used to pitch tents all over the beach to vacation here, and they called it a tent city."

"I guess I should feel lucky to be in a hotel. Harry, what's that strange boat...or is it a plane? Over there in the bay."

"Isn't that amazing? It's amphibious. It's a boat and an airplane, all in one. One of the sailors here told me it's called the G-21, or the Flying Goose."

"That was pretty smart of the Navy to build a combination boat and plane."

"It wasn't built by the Navy, but by Grumman Aircraft before the war. A group of Manhattan millionaires living on Long Island wanted an easier way to commute to work. They financed Grumman to have the amphibian built. These businessmen would leave from the water right near their Long Island mansions and fly as commuters to a seaplane base right at the foot of Wall Street."

"The plane's so big. Do you know how many people it holds?"

"I heard it holds eight passengers and two pilots. One of the officers told me the military had over 300 built for fast transportation to remote locations during this war."

We lounged on our towels at the beach, soaking up the Catalina sun and waiting for it to get warm enough to dive into the ocean water.

"Better cover up in that knockout bathing suit, Kitty. All the men will swarm over here."

I sat up to adjust my swimsuit, and looked toward the pier. "Oh my God—a fire!"

Harry laughed. "That's the Maritime Service conducting a flaming water drill. Gasoline's burned on the surface of the water and the crewmen dive off that pier and push the burning water away. Then they come up for air as soon as possible and swim to safety."

I was awestruck watching sailor after sailor diving into the flaming sea. Black, billowing clouds formed at the water's surface, then stretched high above into the sky.

Courtesy Catalina Island Museum

On our way back to the hotel to get ready for dinner and the dance, we stopped at the ship landing. The performers for the USO show that night had arrived, and were disembarking onto the steamer dock. The women had stylish victory roll hairdos and some had on two-tone heels. They all wore the latest framed sunglasses. One performer had a fur coat on, which seemed ridiculous in the island climate. There were crowds of military men bending and peeping, everyone trying to see who the famous stars were.

Courtesy Catalina Island Museum

"Oh, Harry! I think I saw Bing Crosby and Frances Langford!"

Harry chuckled. "Maybe that was them. I guess we'll find out soon enough."

That night it was albacore again at the Atwater cafeteria, but I didn't care. All I could think about was what movie stars I would see at the casino.

My dress was pretty plain, since I didn't know I'd be ballroom dancing, but then it didn't seem to matter because there was such a shortage of women on the island. Most of the females there were military wives or daughters. They volunteered their time at the Red Cross station, folding bandages to be shipped off for wounded soldiers in battle zones.

Chapter 22
The Blimp

We arrived early in order to enjoy the ambiance of the ballroom before it got too crowded. A handsome captain decked out in his dress uniform offered to show us around.

"Wrigley first built the Sugarloaf Casino in 1920. Have you heard of him?"

Harry answered, "Yes, I'm stationed here and I've told my sister all about him."

"Anyway," the captain continued, "the first casino was too small for the island's growing population, so in 1928 it was torn down. It was moved to Avalon Canyon and was used as an aviary in the bird park. Have you seen the bird park?"

We both shook our heads.

"You should go see it. The aviary's on many acres with over 8,000 rare and exotic birds. It was the world's largest until the war broke out."

"I love birds." I looked him over, admiring his dress uniform.

"The casino is a ballroom stacked over a movie theater. The rock out there was blasted away for the ocean view."

"Do you know how long it took for it to be rebuilt?" Harry inquired.

"About 14 months, working around the clock. I heard it cost about two million dollars."

Harry whistled a soft whistle over that remark.

"Let's go up to the ballroom. It's a beauty." The captain led us up the plushly carpeted, sweeping staircase.

We stood in the middle of the huge ballroom.

"This must hold a lot of people," I exclaimed, waving my arm.

"I think it has a capacity of over 3,000 people." The captain leaned against one of the many outside supporting pillars.

I gazed at the rose-hued walls, black Art Deco reliefs, and the arching 50-foot ceiling with five Tiffany chandeliers. The elevated stage had raised seating areas around the dance floor, and a full-service bar in back. It was magnificent.

"Have you been downstairs to the theater?"

"We sure have, to see the boxing match." Harry placed his hands on his waist.

"Great match that was," the captain said, then added, "the Avalon Theater can seat almost 1,000 people and it's so well insulated you can't even hear the band playing or the dancers on the floor above."

I interrupted the captain's grand tour. "Tell me, sir, what big band is playing tonight?"

Harry touched the captain's sleeve. "Don't tell her. I want it to be a surprise."

The captain smiled. "Oh, you'll be surprised all right."

We all looked toward the ballroom stage when the band entered and began to tune up. Then, right before my inexperienced eyes appeared a man I swore was the famous Bing Crosby.

A little while later, after most of the guests had poured in, the white-fur-clad woman from the dock announced from the microphone, "Ladies and gentlemen, Bing Crosby!"

I swooned along with all the other gals.

"May I have this dance?" The captain led me onto the dance floor.

It was a heavenly acoustic experience, like he had said. The chandelier at the apex of the ballroom displayed a variety of colored lights, enhancing the mood of the entire event. We had an energetic dance to Bing Crosby's famous "Victory Polka" song.

When Bing began to croon "As Time Goes By," Harry cut in. I could tell he was trying to protect my marriage. Bing Crosby's singing style was emotional and very intimate. Tears formed in my eyes when my brother and I danced together. It made me miss my Fred; he was always a fabulous dancer. The famous star ended the show with the last song, "Yankee Doodle Dandy." Everyone joined in, uniting us all in patriotism.

On the walk back to my hotel, Harry told me that Bing Crosby was the most recognized celebrity who had done the most for the morale of the American G.I. He had traveled all over Europe entertaining the troops. Bing Crosby also learned how to pronounce German from written scripts, and would read propaganda broadcasts intended for the German forces. His radio name was "Der Bingle."

"He was a knockout to hear and see. I'll never forget this night out, Harry, never!"

"You wouldn't believe the list of stars that have entertained on this island." Harry rattled off the long list of stars. "Jimmy Dorsey, Benny Goodman, Glenn Miller, Harry James, Abbott and Costello, Kate Smith, Rudy Vallée, Cary Grant, and Bob Hope have all performed here."

We meandered down the path in the starlit night to have a cup of coffee at the Busy Bee All-Night Café. The sky was ever so bright due to the enforced blackout from the war. It was Harry's last night on leave, and mine. The fog had crept in like a mysterious ghost. I was glad I had my jacket on.

All of a sudden, we heard air raid sirens in the hills, and saw fiery flashes, which was startling against the darkness of the town.

"Something terrible must be happening. I've gotta get back to my base. You'd better stay in your room, Sis. I'll see you off on the steamship tomorrow. Goodnight." Harry rushed off to find out about the fire.

I stood outside the Hotel Atwater, staring up through the thick fog as fire spread throughout the mountain. It took a while to get to sleep with all the commotion.

Once asleep, I had a nasty nightmare that the island was bombarded by Japanese planes landing high in the mountains. They also landed in

Two Harbors and Harry had to fight them away with a knife. I awoke with a moan and rubbed the sweat on my forehead with the pillow. I sat up and listened for more sirens. When I heard none, I tossed and turned until morning.

The next morning I threw on some clothes and hightailed it to the Busy Bee to see if I could get the news. There was plenty of buzz from all the people there. All I could hear were the words "crash," "blimp," and "death."

Harry showed up. "There you are. Did you hear what happened?"

"I've been trying to figure it out."

"The fire was from a blimp crash."

"What's a blimp?"

"You know, like the Goodyear blimp. This one was even larger."

"Was it a Japanese blimp?" I gripped the counter and swiveled on my stool.

"No, it was our Naval airship. It watches for Japanese subs because blimps can fly very low. Catalina is so vulnerable to attack that there are many blimps patrolling the island. I heard at my base that it was the heavy fog that caused the accident. I'm sorry to say that some of the passengers were killed."

"How tragic." I breathed a sigh of relief that the Japanese hadn't invaded the island, like I had dreamed.

Later that day, Harry picked up a copy of the *Catalina Islander.*

CATALINA ISLANDER
Five Killed! U.S. Navy Blimp Crashes!
Five crewmen were burned to death, with five seriously injured, when the Navy blimp crashed into the mountain hillside at the south end of Avalon last night.

The Naval airship, K-111, took off from Del Mar, California. This airship was 246 feet long, with a height of 70 feet. The gondola was 40 feet long, and had two Pratt & Whitney engines. It struck the Catalina mountain carrying

700 gallons of fuel. This was a night navigation flight to conduct a 22-hour training operation employed by the United States Navy for anti-submarine patrol.

Visibility was very limited by weather as the blimp hit the Palisades ridge on the island. The impact ignited its fuel tanks and the flaming airship caused a brush fire of over two acres. The K-111 was left in smoldering ruins and was a total loss. The surrounding mountains were illuminated, despite the wet fog, for more than two hours. Debris was hurled to the bottom of the 600-foot-deep canyon.

Rescue crews with packhorses and stretchers worked all night to bring out the airship crew. The injured were carried off to the U.S. Maritime Hospital.

The names of the deceased will not be publicly listed until the cause of the catastrophe can be investigated and the next of kin notified.

"The talk at the base was that the pilot did not ascertain the correct height of the mountain range. The heavy fog left zero visibility and he did not ensure sufficient altitude to clear it." Harry tightened his fists.

"What a tragedy that five men died. I wonder if the other five will survive?"

"I heard that one is burned too severely to make it."

"Maybe the Navy should stop using the blimps."

"This is the only crash that has ever occurred during the war."

The catastrophic event of the previous night dampened my joyous vacation on the island, and the reality of war penetrated my thoughts. I went back to the hotel to pack my bag. Gloominess pervaded me. I slowly put on my tight-fitting uniform.

Harry was quiet, not his usual self, as we weaved through all the servicemen walking toward the *USS Avalon*. I wondered if we were sharing the same thoughts. Would we all survive this horrific war?

Chapter 23
Beaulieu, England

I took a troop ship to London, England after my stay on Catalina Island. The train ride to Beaulieu was another 80-mile journey. The country trip to the finishing school was a pleasure after being in bombed-out London. Even though the Blitz was over, there were still piles of rubble and several churches still in ruins. Makeshift scaffolding surrounded some of the devastated buildings. St. Paul's Cathedral and the Bank of England seemed unscathed, but many houses had been destroyed. Of course, nothing could be rebuilt with the war raging on in all the other countries. It was frightening to see in person, even though Fred and I had read about it.

After getting off the train at Beaulieu in south England, a friendly soldier from the finishing school picked me up in a large Army truck with canvas-covered sides.

"Hi, code name's Allen. Let me help you with your bag. Welcome to the New Forest."

"Nice to meet you, Allen."

"Make sure you use your *nom de guerre* at all times. It's Kitty, isn't it?" Allen sped out into the country, the truck bouncing on the rough road.

"Yes. How long will it take to get to the school?" My exhaustion was beginning to show and I rubbed my eyes.

"It's not too far. Don't worry, you'll have a day to settle in after your long journey, then the chief instructor will come by to give you your course content with its aims."

A 5x5 sign appeared. We came to a sudden stop.

HALT!
CONTROL POST
RESTRICTED ZONE

The guard in the post came out, poked his head through the truck window, gave me a suspicious look, and demanded my passport. He looked it over twice, and stared at me for a minute before saying, "Proceed."

We drove through a rich green pine forest.

"We're almost to where you'll be staying. This part of the property is Beaulieu Manor, where Lord Montagu resides. The SOE has requisitioned all the other houses on the property for the finishing school."

My eyes feasted all over the beautiful Victorian country mansion. Indeed, it held true to its French meaning, which was "beautiful place." The stately palace, with its molded archways, enormous terraced stained glass windows on the towers, and turrets, was a fanciful experience to see. The many large chimneys, topped with decorative pots on steep pitched roofs, were a sight to behold. All around the stately home were glorious grounds with gardens, expansive lawns, and walkways overlooking the Beaulieu River. Upon closer viewing, I noticed some of the flowers were too leggy and were starting to seed. Many of the bushes grew wild, while some retained their sculpted, topiary shapes.

Wartime must be taking its toll on the maintenance of this huge property, I thought. "How many acres does the finishing school have?"

"About 10,000 acres make up the Beaulieu Estate. The finishing school uses all of it except where Lord Montagu resides. The manor was once a 13th-century gatehouse of the Beaulieu Abbey, which is in ruins."

We rode past the front corner of the estate. The entire structure looked like an ancient stone castle, except for a small Tudor front that seemed out of place, haphazardly stuck to the mansion. Its white stucco with wide, dark, crisscrossing wood contrasted sharply with the natural gray stone.

The Army officer drove up a long track through a narrow woodland road beyond Beaulieu Manor. The summer sunlight dimmed through the heavy forest of pine trees.

"Here's the Boarsman House. An instructor will pay you a visit with your syllabus of classes tomorrow. Good luck!"

I got my bags out and before I could say thank you, he sped off through the forest. His parting words, "good luck," made me feel concerned about the unknown events that lay ahead.

My beautiful vacation in Catalina became a distant memory when I walked with hesitation into the building. Boarsman House looked modern, a typical English-style building, but there were several bright and airy rooms that gave it a Scandinavian design. Through one of the windows I noticed an unkempt tennis court overlooking a field that sloped down to a horseshoe-shaped lake.

I found the room the soldier had directed me to, and placed a timid knock on the door. A slight, small woman around my age opened it. *"Bonjour."*

"Bonjour," I answered.

"I was told I'd have a roommate. My name's Nnn…I mean, my code name's Madeleine," she continued in French.

"Glad to meet you. Call me Kitty. Do you speak English?"

"Yes, but most everyone here at Boarsman House speaks French." Madeleine spoke in a quiet, breathless way.

"That's good, I need to perfect my accent."

"Your accent's not too bad. I'm about to go to dinner. I'll show you where the dining room is." Madeleine went to the closet and put on a brown sweater over a khaki-colored uniform made for men. "You're welcome to put your bags in the closet until you have time to unpack. Tell me, Kitty, what's your specialty?"

"If you mean which class did I do best in at basic training, it's transmitting."

"I thought it would be. Most of us here at Boarsman House are wireless transmitter operators. What's your speed?"

I leaned in closer in order to hear her soft voice. "About 18 words per minute."

"You're good. It's better than mine."

At the dining hall we had an outstanding French meal, reminding me of my college days at the Sorbonne. "These vegetables taste very fresh."

"Oh, they are. We are very fortunate to be excluded from rationing here. The SOE has retained Lord Montagu's gardener and we have wonderful food. Pheasants are hunted on a regular basis and served. Will you be going to Ringway Airfield to practice jumping?"

"I hope not. I didn't do very well trying to jump from a practice tower at Camp X in Canada." My face flushed from the thought.

"I'll be happy to show you around Beaulieu on Sunday, when we have a day off."

"That would be wonderful. How big is this entire SOE camp, anyway?"

"There are many schools in houses spread all over the acreage. Some of them are quite luxurious. Beaulieu is called the jewel in the crown of all the SOE training schools."

"Oh, my. How can we get around?"

"Bicycles are the best way."

The next day, Madeleine went to her classes while I waited for a commander to come by with my schedule. On Madeleine's desk I noticed a thin book, *Twenty Indian Tales*, by Noor Singh. I flipped through the children's book. It was about Buddha and India. I spent the rest of the time reading one of Major Fearless's books, *Defendu: Scientific Self-defense*, which was underneath the children's book.

A knock sounded. I straightened my skirt, refreshed my lipstick, and opened the door.

The commander spoke in English. "You've been placed at Boarsman House for two reasons. Most every woman here is proficient in wireless training and most are French. Because you are an American, we wanted your accent to be perfect before being sent on an assignment." He switched to French. "Your behavior will be watched at all times during your six weeks of final training. These are the rules here: never expose your real name or background to anyone, speak in French at all times, don't get drunk in public or sleep with another agent-in-training—or anyone, for that matter." He glared at my breasts.

I pulled at my blouse to make myself look smaller.

The bald man's steel gray eyes pierced through mine like straight pins jabbing into a pincushion. "I must warn you to decide now if you want to attend finishing school, because if you begin and don't complete the courses, you will be sent to the Cooler."

"The what?" I gave him an incredulous stare.

"The Cooler, or Inverie House. It is in the highlands of Scotland. Its remote location makes it reachable only by motorboat. Incompetent or unlucky agents are held there until their knowledge of secrets can no longer endanger the operations of the war." The commander paused, waiting for any reaction. "Are you ready to sign the Official Secrets Act?"

"Yes." I signed the form, which was identical to the one I had signed at Camp X.

"Here's your syllabus. If you pass all your classes you will be sent to the London office to be evaluated, and perhaps then you will be given a mission. Any questions?"

Before I could answer, he turned away from me and placed the syllabus on the desk. I did have a question, but felt too intimidated by his manner and shook my head no. He left without another word.

I read the syllabus, titled "Advanced Wireless Training, Make-up and Disguise, Silent Killing, and Survival." I scanned the paper again, looking for parachute training. My records from Camp X with my failure at the jump tower must have been sent to Beaulieu. I grasped the schedule firmly. All the classes were there at Boarsman House and I assumed they were all conducted in French.

I went to the room listed to get my uniform. No one was there. Under a sign that read "Battle Dress" I found a men's small size pair of pants and a large shirt. It was comfy to get back into pants again, reminding me of basic training.

After changing, I went outside and strolled through the enchanting forest. Lush vegetation surrounded me, full of fern fronds, tiny bluebells, and budding yellow iris. The fresh air intoxicated my senses. I took deep breaths and enjoyed myself, especially after experiencing the musty, moldy smell of bombed-out London while waiting for my train. After walking about a mile, I headed back. I was anxious about my classes and decided to attend the last two.

The Silent Killing class was on the top floor of Boarsman House. After taking an empty seat, I was quite surprised to see so many women, unlike at Camp X. The instructor was Major Fearless, my basic training weapons professor in Canada. His hair seemed to have receded further since I had seen him last.

Major Fearless began the lecture in impeccable French. I took notes.

"The principal object of this course is to kill and to kill silently. There can always be a moment when you're caught without a firearm or may be unable to use it because it would raise alarm. Always remember, this is a war we are fighting, and not a sport. The aim is to kill your opponent as quickly as possible. Attack their weakest points and don't ever give them a chance to attack yours." The major raised his voice. "Silent killing is NOT a technique, it is a state of mind! I'll be teaching you about unarmed combat. By practicing my methods, you will learn how to take care of yourself, no matter how big your adversary is. You will be instructed in Judo. This is an extension of Jiu-jitsu first developed by ancient Lama Chinese monks to protect themselves from robbers. I used to work for the Shanghai Municipal Police Department. After being severely attacked and ending up in the hospital, I took up Jiu-jitsu. The Japanese perfected it by adding over 300 additional holds and throws. After years of private instruction, I received my black belt. The armed forces of several nations now train men to use Jiu-jitsu as a weapon of protection. By learning Judo, you can take down any enemy, male or female, by surprise and ward off an attacker with a variety of moves."

Inside the door was that sign I had seen at my interview and at my previous weapons class: *Know Yourself... Know Your Weapon... Know Your Enemy.*

"First we will practice with dummies, then with each other. I will teach you all how to kick, the use of open hand, chin jabs, and body holds. You will learn how to defend yourself using a knee, the head, elbows, and the fingertips. Further classes will be in knife fighting."

One woman in the front row murmured, "Uh-oh."

The major added, "The knife fighting will be practiced by using short pieces of thick rope on dummies. Because there is a shortage of rubber, we don't have rubber knives. Class, pair off on the mats."

All the women seemed to gravitate toward each other. One fellow started to approach me, but I was relieved when a tall gal got to me first.

The major demonstrated all the jabs and body holds very carefully, not once hurting his opponent.

Jacqueline was my new partner, and much to my surprise, we had fun copying and trying out all the defensive moves the major demonstrated.

"Tomorrow I will be matching you up in unequal sizes. Remember, practice, practice, practice! Dismissed!"

Oh no, not that expression again...

Even though it was true, I was tired of hearing those words—but then I guess I was just plain tired, anyway. My confidence began to diminish. I wondered if women would be paired with the men in tomorrow's Judo instruction.

Chapter 24
Finishing School

*O*ne more class, then I'll be ready for some shut-eye.
I sat in the Make-up and Disguise workshop waiting for the instructor. It was very rude of him to be this late. After all, we were expected to be on time. There were about 50 of us packed into the lounge area.

In burst a small man wearing a hat, shouting, "You have five minutes to write down my description!" He left immediately.

All the men laughed, while the gals wrote fast. I didn't remember much, but I jotted a few things down: small man, black hair, no uniform, brown hat. That was the best I could recall, since he had caught us off-guard.

The teacher came back in, went around and snatched up all the papers, and threw them on the front desk. Off went his black hat, and he rubbed his sideburns with a cloth, revealing his blond hair. I deduced that I had written brown hat instead of black because it had looked like my father's.

"That, class, was your first test. As a potential agent you must keep your wits about you at all times by being highly observant, just as the enemy would be toward you. You will learn in this class that disguise does not mean simply covering your face with a lot of make-up."

The teacher brought out a suitcase, removed from it an odd assortment of articles, and arranged them on the large desk. "Here before you are ordinary items that can be used for emergency disguises when you are on a mission and need to change your appearance."

Displayed on the desk before us were charcoal, tweezers, small metal nuts, sponges, a comb, a brush, pencils, burned corks, a few stones, newspaper, cotton, bleach, a box of matches, cigarettes, an ashtray, eyeglasses, iodine, and peroxide.

"Charcoal, a used wooden match, burnt cork, or a soft leaded pencil can all be used to darken your hair. First, rub it in, then lightly comb through. Apply it several times. A used wooden match or pencil can also be worked into the lines or wrinkles in your face to deepen them and develop circles under your eyes. This method ages you. A pencil can also be used to thicken your eyebrows. Tweezers can be used to thin them, making your eyes seem farther apart. Here are a few more tricks." He stuffed two small metal nuts into each nostril.

"See my big nose?" He let out a silly chuckle. He lit a cigarette and placed it on the ashtray. While it burned, he tore off pieces from a sponge and stuffed them into his cheeks, altering his facial contours. After the cigarette had left a pile of ashes, the teacher rubbed them into his hair, giving it a gray appearance. "Class, hair can be changed easily. Long hair can be shortened, made tidy, or untidy."

He took the comb and changed his hair. "Even the simple method of changing your part can make you look different. Now, before your mission, it's a good time to grow your hair longer than normal because cutting it can alter your appearance. Peroxide or bleach can be bought to lighten hair. Pour it into a saucer and apply it with a small toothbrush. It will take an hour to dry on your hair. Women who have long bobs can put their hair up or slick it straight back into either a knot or roll. Add a ribbon, bow, wig, or false braid, and *voilà!* A new disguise."

He was quite a jokester during the lecture, and his hands flew about when he spoke, adding to his act. The teacher untied his shoe, placed something in it, and put it back on.

"Small stones placed in one shoe can cause you to limp, but it is most important to *remember* to limp. Add inches to your height by folding a newspaper to form a ramp in the heel of your shoe."

We were all very impressed with the transformation as he limped around the classroom with a hunched back. He switched from French to a British accent and mannerisms. He hoisted up his trousers and tightened his belt, making him look taller. Most of the class laughed with glee.

The instructor silenced everyone by declaring, "I know I'm a good actor, but this class is no joke. Pay attention and listen, because it could save your life."

A fellow in the front row raised his hand. "Umm, sir, what about growing a beard?"

The teacher answered with his high, effeminate voice, "My code name's Paul. Good question. Beards can take 25-40 days to grow and mustaches 15-25. A man changing his facial hair is a perfect disguise. Even changing the shape of a mustache works well. Don't forget you can darken or lighten facial hair and use false whiskers. Make an unshaven appearance with brown make-up by applying with small pieces of porous sponge. For a fresh, younger face, a close shave is necessary. Use hot towels and alum, which will tighten the skin; then apply talcum powder."

Paul took a bottle of iodine and cotton, swabbed some on his teeth, and presented a nasty-looking smile to the class. A few people snickered. We were all enjoying this highly entertaining lecture.

"For an appearance that looks like you've come from the country or work in a factory, don't forget to roughen up your hands with oil and dirt. Make a few cuts, and be sure your fingernails are dirty. This makes a hard-worked look. The way to make smooth hands is to put ladies' face powder on them. Skin color can be changed by using the surface of an old piece of rusty iron, like the fume vent of a water heater. When on a mission, sometimes it's necessary to be creative and avail oneself of whatever is around. To change a cleft chin, wax mixed with a little rouge can be worked into the cleft to make it disappear. Scars may be covered up by buying colloid at the chemists or a hospital. To make scars, colloid is applied to the skin with a brush, and held in place for 1 ½ minutes to dry. Remember, class, make-up and disguise must be used in case of emergency and for self-protection; external imitation is not sufficient.

You must imitate the character effectively in every way; the walk, voice, and mannerisms. To mentally prepare yourself, sit down, gather your thoughts about your new personality and don't come out of character. Hold your cigarette another way, stand taller or slump, tilt your head when you talk. To stand up straight, a strong figure-eight cord crossed on your back will remind you to throw out your chest, making you appear taller. Change your gait, gestures, and your reactions. If you tell a lie often enough, you begin to believe it yourself. When you work hard on being a Dr. Jekyll or Mr. Hyde, you can become that character. The enemy is sharp, but is indeed human and can be fooled. When on an assignment, if you can, keep several disguises with you—caps, hats, rough gardening clothes, suede shoes. It's best to stay in crowds and inconspicuously try to blend in. If you are sent on a mission, you may be equipped with a new past, present, and physical appearance. A good background cover is hard to build up and can be easily destroyed."

Paul paused and took a sip of water. "Your homework for tonight is to look in your bedroom mirror and study yourself. Everyone has peculiar, individual mannerisms. Analyze and eliminate these. There are many classes of society that all sit, stand, and walk in their own particular way. Learn to take on a new persona. Tomorrow I will choose a few of you to present your new identities. Have a good evening. Class dismissed." Paul placed all his equipment in his bag and left in a hurry.

Even though I had been stimulated by the disguise lecture, my adrenaline level wound down. I was glad to go back to my room for a good night's sleep.

Madeleine gave me a warm welcome. "*Bonjour.* I see you went to class instead of taking the day off. How was it?"

"It was nice to get back into class again. The lecture on disguise was so interesting. The teacher had an abundance of tricks for how to change your appearance."

"I heard that Paul's a famous actor that the school hired. He knows everything about make-up and disguise. I enjoyed that class. What an entertainer—a good nightclub act! Let's go to dinner."

"I think I'd rather go to bed. I'm pretty exhausted."

"Suit yourself. See you in the morning."

Chapter 25
Biking Around
the New Forest

I awoke in the morning, sat up, and rubbed my eyes while I watched Madeleine write in her small notebook in her beautiful, spidery handwriting.

I got my clothes from the closet and noticed on the top shelf there were many books with the last name Singh.

"You sure have quite a collection of books."

"I'm an author, and my father was, too."

The children's book I saw on the desk must be one of hers, I thought. It seemed to me that she was exposing her real identity, which gave me an uncomfortable feeling.

"What classes do you have today, Madeleine?"

"I'm done with my classes and am trying to get my speed up on transmitting. I can't seem to get past the minimum words per minute."

"It does take constant practice. My 18 WPM makes me feel quite satisfied, which I think is why I got accepted into finishing school. Will you be assigned a mission soon?"

"Yes, I have an appointment with the SOE officer, Miss Armstrong, in London in a few weeks." Madeleine made spiral doodles in the corners of her book while she spoke. She closed it up. "Let's go to breakfast."

We went off to eat and had a scrumptious French breakfast of crepes with fresh-picked wild berries. Madeleine told me the gardener picked them in the woods daily.

In the advanced wireless transmitting class I found a seat in the front and Madeleine went to the back of the classroom to practice.

The teacher wrote his name on the blackboard, "Yorkie," then underneath put a long list of letters followed by their meanings. He pointed and recited each one. "QRK: How are you receiving me? QSA: This should be your answer, followed by a number from one to five. Over three means fairly audible," he added. "QTC: I have a message for you. QRU: I have nothing more. QRS: send slower. VA: close down. QUA: This means there is immediate danger and you are forced to stop transmitting, that there is probably sudden enemy exposure."

Yorkie shouted out each code for us to type as fast as we could. Then he added a phrase: "I have a message for you."

We looked at the board and typed out QTC. The sound of my key beeping was sharp and piercing, like a frightened mouse trapped in a corner, protesting.

"Class, continue on your own. You must practice every day in order to get your speed up to at least 20 words a minute. Remember, we are policemen of the airwaves and have a very important job. Tomorrow I will demonstrate how to repair and reconstruct a damaged radio with makeshift parts. This is in case your set becomes impaired after parachuting in."

My teeth gritted together upon hearing the word "parachuting." I tried to put it out of my mind.

I practiced transmitting with a trainer back in my room for an hour, and was pleased with my progress. Madeleine came in and I almost said hello, then remembered I was to speak French at all times.

At last Sunday arrived—a much-needed day off. Madeleine and I went biking all over Beaulieu, like she had promised. Our bikes rattled when we crossed over the metal bars of the cattle guard, vibrating the wheels. We sped down the long, private road where there were many houses hidden in the deep woods of the New Forest.

"How many houses make up the finishing school?" I caught my breath.

"There are 12 spread out all over the 10,000 acres. I'll show you a few."

The ride was exhilarating, with my hair blowing freely in the breeze, and the stress of classes behind me. A motorcycle roared down the hill.

"Pedal fast!" Madeleine was breathing hard. "He might report us."

When the sound of the motorcycle disappeared, she slowed down and pointed. "Over there's Inchmery House, or STS 38. The SOE almost placed me there with the Free French paratroopers in training, but they wanted me to perfect my wireless transmitting skills instead."

"Who are they?"

"They are the first SOE agents to be parachuted into France."

I got that tight, lead-ball feeling in the bottom of my belly every time the word "parachute" was mentioned, and was glad my wireless training was coming along so well. The ride out toward the Beaulieu River was a joy, with the summer sun spreading warmth on my face.

On the opposite end of the river, Madeleine waved her hand at the House on the Shore. "The gardener lives near there. Over that way, on the west bank of the river, is the Drokes. It has 13 bedrooms, and two cottages on 24 acres. Most of the houses are segregated into national groups. The finishing school placed the Dutch in the House on the Shore, overlooking the water, no doubt to help them feel more at home. It's situated right on the coast at the head of the beach because it's a prime defensive point. The residents are required to be ready for any attempts at an enemy landing. The Norwegians overlook the Solent, but it's too far for us to bicycle to."

"Do you know how many nationalities the finishing school has here?"

"I've figured out that there's Italian, Spanish, Dutch, Norwegian, Poles, French, and of course, British. There aren't many Americans."

"I guess I'm lucky that the school has accepted me. It's very peaceful here." Resting my bicycle on the bank, I sprawled out on the lawn and twisted the grass in my fingers. I pulled a blade and tickled it under my nose, enjoying the fragrance.

Madeleine sat next to me. "I find it delightful to ride out here every Sunday. It's hard to imagine that just across the Solent is the bomb-torn port of Southampton."

"I was in London last week on my way here and was overcome by what the Germans have done to the city. It was a beautiful place when I stayed there during my college years."

"I was raised in London. It's shocking to see it now. This is why we're preparing ourselves to help win this God-awful war, don't you think?" Madeleine brushed a strand of her black hair as a breeze came up.

"When I saw the dreadful condition of London, it did reinforce my conviction to do my part, like my husband and brother signed up to do." My words caught in my throat as the sadness of missing my family suddenly overcame me.

"Are they in the service?"

"Yes, they're both in the Army. I don't even know where they're stationed now. It's been hard to maintain contact since I've been traveling. Maybe we should go back. What did you mean when you said you hoped the man on the motorcycle wouldn't report us?"

"We're not supposed to know about the other schools or wander around."

"I didn't know that. The commanding officer didn't mention it to me. How did you find out so much about the grounds here?"

"Some of us talk in private. I admit, I am a very curious person."

"I'm ready to head back." I got up and mounted my bike.

"Follow me, then." Madeleine rode ahead.

After catching up with her, I observed, "The houses seem to all be different sizes."

"Yes, they do vary. Some have a few bedrooms, with 20 at the most. STS 36 had the first batch of women to be trained at Beaulieu."

"What's 36?"

"That's another name for our house. All the houses are numbered. STS means Special Training School. Over there's Vineyard House."

Vines entwined all over the walls of the stone house, decorating it with a lovely maze of branches.

"Tell me, Madeleine, are there any women instructors at Beaulieu?"

"No, just secretaries. They live at the main headquarters. The Rings are a mile to the south end, where most of the instructors live in 39 rooms on 15 acres. I find the teachers a pretty fishy odd lot, don't you?"

I thought about Paul, the disguise instructor, then Major Fearless, and nodded in agreement.

Madeleine slowed down. "I know for a fact that one teacher was a professional burglar and safebreaker who was recently released from prison to teach. Most of the housemasters are veterans of the First World War, and they sure are funny old dug-ups."

I snickered, enjoying Madeleine's British expressions.

The ride back was delightful. I was able to identify the various trees along the way: sycamore, ash, birch, and alder. The smell of the forest as we sped down the pathways was intoxicating.

Chapter 26
Jacqueline

O n Monday, I had to hunt all over the property for what was called "Survival Class." It met deep in the woods. The name of the class filled me with anxiety. The captain was a heavy, burly man with a pockmarked complexion and a rich, resonant voice.

"This may be the most important class that you will attend at Beaulieu. Your lives will depend on it. Everyone pay close attention," he barked. "We are living in a vulnerable area for attack by the Nazis, being right on the coast. If we were to be bombed, I would expect you all to follow my procedures in how to survive. This class will help when you are sent on a mission, because anything can happen and you must be prepared. Here, right in the floor of the New Forest, we have constructed hideouts—large holes in the ground that you might have all walked over and not even detected. These hideouts are large enough to house a stay-behind party with all their food, weapons, and ammunition. We can then emerge at night to attach limpet mines with delayed fuses to the tracks of German tanks and vehicles."

He paused, his eyes boring into each of our faces gathered in front of him. "I'm a former gamekeeper and I'll teach you how to trap and poach game. Here in the forest we will snare rabbits and hedgehogs. I will also teach you how to fish in the river. You will learn how to sustain yourself with fruit, herbs, and stinging nettles. It is crucial to identify what is edible and what is poisonous. You will learn how to live off the land if you have to, for weeks on end."

The skilled woodsman continued, "I will prepare you for your mission ahead, how to steal chickens and livestock without alerting the owners, then how to strip them in preparation for eating." He paused again when my face displayed a startled appearance.

We spent an hour hiking through the tall bracken and yellow-flowered gorse while Captain Clark pointed out hidden ponds and bogs. In a far-off field I spied wild ponies grazing the land. There was an abundance of animal and insect life that the captain scouted out. The next day he would take us on pheasant and duck shoots. The following week would focus more on fishing, including how to stun salmon and sea trout with hand grenades.

I was full of anxiety in Judo class. Major Fearless had us pair off in unequal sizes. He either had a man pair with a girl or a small person with a larger person.

"No matter how big your adversary, if you pay attention and learn all I have to teach, you will be able to take care of yourself using unarmed combat. But, keep in mind that you will receive no credit if you kill or damage your sparring partner!"

This gave the class a good chuckle.

We learned how to flip each other, and to sweep a partner's leg, causing them to lose their balance. It was all about leverage, not about how big a person was or whether they were a heavyweight. We were taught to push our opponent's knee with the bottom of a foot, and even how to use our hip to throw a person over. I had the same partner again, the striking, tall gal with a charming native French accent named Jacqueline. She was very athletic and I was grateful for her assistance in this challenging class. Much to my surprise, I was able to throw her over with my hip.

She got up and praised me. *"Très bien!"*

Judo seemed almost magical and I couldn't believe the feats that we were able to perform.

Jacqueline and I went to dinner together. I filled my plate with an assortment of garden vegetables and pheasant again. In a corner of the large room sat Madeleine, reading a book while eating.

"Let's go sit with my roommate, Madeleine. I'll introduce her to you."

"Mais, oui, I know Madeleine. We were in FANY together."

Jacqueline kissed both of Madeleine's cheeks.

"Adèle, it is so good to see you again," Madeleine said.

Jacqueline looked around and whispered, "My code name's Jacqueline."

"Oh, yes."

The two friends spoke in rapid French, going over all their adventures in the FANY.

I listened in and learned FANY stood for First Aid Nursing Yeomanry. During this war the yeomanry did an assortment of volunteer jobs, including helping in canteens, guarding prisoners of war, working in ambulance crews, and were military transport drivers.

I was surprised to learn that in the FANY women were commissioned officers and were allowed to carry weapons. Madeleine and Jacqueline had driven an ambulance together. The conversation made me think about my roommate, Germaine; she had been a FANY ambulance driver even with her false foot. I hoped she was well and safe.

"Jacqueline, what made you join the SOE? The last time I saw you I thought you married that French Foreign Legion officer, became pregnant, then quit the yeomanry" Madeleine searched Jacqueline's down-turned face.

With her eyes staring at the table, Jacqueline choked out, "My husband died in action near El Alamein. Our beautiful baby girl was barely four months old when he was killed." After one tear dripped down into her plate, Madeleine reached over and held her hand.

Jacqueline brushed her tears away. "I joined the SOE because being a mother was not enough for me, and I desperately needed something to live for. I am fortunate that my mother is able to care for my baby. I will do anything to free France from the Nazis—to vindicate my husband's death." She sniffled and squeezed each finger on her hand.

A silence hung over us, even though the mess hall was buzzing with activity.

I broke our sad silence. "How are your other classes coming along? You are so skilled in Judo, I love being your partner."

"Thanks," she said, cheering up a bit. "I'm doing very well in my parachute class. Next week, I'm being dropped into an unknown area miles from the camp, then tested to see if I can figure out how to return with speed and safety." Jacqueline's face lit up.

I was glad to have changed the subject, knowing death could knock at my door anytime. After all, my small family now consisted of only my brother and husband, who were both in the war.

"You mean dropped by airplane?" Madeleine inquired.

"No, by truck in the dead of night. We are all dropped separately, dressed in jumpsuits and parachute harnesses. Then we have to take them off, dig a hole, and bury them without a trace. After leaving the drop zone, my assignment is to find a specific location in the dark. It's training for when I'll be parachuted into France. By the way, I haven't seen either of you in any of my parachute classes. How come?"

"I will not parachute and I'm deathly afraid of heights. I made that very clear to the officer in charge in basic training. Fortunately, because I passed all my classes, they let me continue on to Beaulieu."

Jacqueline looked in my direction. "Have you taken any parachute training classes, Kitty?"

"I did at Camp X. I'm embarrassed to say that I didn't complete them because I was afraid of breaking an ankle. One of the gals actually did. I guess Beaulieu accepted me because I did so well in all the other classes." I changed the subject. "Good luck on your nighttime drop zone assignment. I hope it doesn't take you too long to find your way. You've taken the survival class, haven't you?" I took a bite of bread.

"*Oui,* that'll be a helpful class for me to draw from. I'll be transferred to Ringway Airfield in Manchester soon after I complete all my tests."

"What'll you being doing there? You don't have to tell me if you're not allowed to." I moved some of the moist pheasant around on my plate.

"Oh, it's not top secret. Some people say you either have to be crazy or drunk to jump out of a plane."

I blanched and Madeleine remained quiet.

Jacqueline continued, "I'll be staying at Dunham House along with the other paratroopers, right near the airfield. At last I'll be training to jump from Tiger Moths and Lysander airplanes instead of that silly jump tower. I'm looking forward to it."

"Sounds frightening to me. Are you afraid at all?"

"*Non.* After all, I'll be wearing a parachute."

"What if it fails to open?" I pursed my lips together.

"I've had 40 hours of instruction on how to pack my own chute. It was a very thorough class on panel folding, line stowing, twist removals, pack sewing, and harnesses. I've been tested on the parts of a parachute and have learned how to pack it so it opens properly after being dropped. Besides, there's a reserve parachute pack if the main chute fails to open. You know, girls, a parachute is easy to open. All you do is pull a handle that sticks out of the right side. The class I took really builds confidence in learning how the chute will operate correctly."

"Aren't you worried about being away from your baby, Jacqueline?" Madeleine asked.

"Of course I miss her, but she is with my mother. After Charles was killed, I've been determined to avenge his death and defend my country." Jacqueline's voice raised an octave higher. "What about you, *Princesse,* what made you sign up for the SOE?"

I interrupted, repeating the French word for princess. "*Princesse?*" I looked Madeleine over. She did look quite exotic with her copper tan skin and black hair.

Jacqueline laughed. "Sitting right here before you is a real *princesse*. Madeleine is a direct descendant of the last Mogul emperor of southern India on her father's side, making her royalty. Her father, who passed away, was a spiritual Sufi leader."

"My mother's American," Madeleine added.

Jacqueline whispered, "Madeleine, I'm surprised to see you here at the SOE finishing school. An ambulance driver is more in line with your religion than becoming a spy. After all, you are a Muslim from a conservative spiritual family."

Madeleine blushed, paused, and glanced out one of the dining room windows. She spoke to her fork. "When my brother joined the RAF and our family was forced out of Paris, I wanted to do something to help my country, as well as the Jewish people. I almost married a Jewish man. The Nazis have no religious harmony. I cannot sit around passively watching them take innocent French Jewish people from their homes. My family had to leave Paris with a quarter of the population still left behind. We had to flee from the Germans and move to London. I still can hear the roar of German Stuka bomber planes in my dreams. I'm determined to return to France and help take it back."

Listening to the convictions of both Jacqueline and Madeleine reinforced my own to win the war. I left the two chums to catch up on their lives, even though I was surprised how much they began disclosing to each other. I knew that it was forbidden to talk about your "real" background, according to the SOE oath. It made me concerned about my roommate. Madeleine seemed so forgetful, the way she forgot code names and left her books around with her real name exposed on them. Maybe she had not been that well trained to be an agent...or was it that her personality was flawed?

I went to the housemaster's room to find out if I had any mail. There in the file cabinet under my code name was a letter from Fred. It was the first time I had seen a V-mail, or Victory Mail letter. I knew the Army censored it, then copied it to film. Then they printed it and mailed it postage free. The V-mail was one sheet of paper, folded a special way so that an envelope was not necessary. I searched through the file cabinet again, hoping for a letter from my brother. I hadn't heard from him for quite a while. When we were in Catalina he was so nonchalant about going to Burma, but I knew it would be a very dangerous mission.

Chapter 27
Letters

Kathleen, my dearest:

I enjoyed reading your letter last month about your vacation on Santa Catalina Island with your brother. I'm glad you were able to get a little holiday after basic training in ~~South Carolina.~~ *I'm wondering how long it will take you to get this letter and where you are stationed now.*

My training to be a ~~glider pilot~~ *is now complete and I am on a mission. The trip here was quite exhausting with the deafening noise of the* ~~canvas-covered glider plane~~ *drumming incessantly throughout the entire* ~~flight.~~ *It makes a horrific pounding sound inside, but is* ~~silent from the enemies~~ *on the outside.*

We were ~~pulled~~ *all the way across the* ~~English Channel~~ *by a* ~~C-47 transport tug plane.~~ *The* ~~tow pilot~~ *tried to warn me how to land my* ~~Waco CG-4A glider~~ *safely, but our communications failed. The delicate* ~~telephone lines~~ *that wrapped around the* ~~tow-rope shorted out~~ *upon being* ~~dragged before takeoff.~~ *In class, we were cautioned that this could happen and were instructed that when the* ~~tow plane lowers its wheels,~~ *that's when it is time to cut loose the* ~~rope.~~ *Thank God I remembered this and landed the* ~~transport glider~~ *at the right time.*

When we landed, our ~~glider plane crashed~~ *helplessly into a potato field. Its* ~~nose~~ *pounded into the ground, the dirt poured into the* ~~plane,~~ *and the* ~~wings~~ *broke off. We were all glad it* didn't ~~flip upside down~~ like one of the other ~~gliders~~ did in the field next to ours. Our troop had to dig our way out of the dirt. Fortunately, we had digging equipment, including a small ~~bulldozer~~ in the ~~glider~~. The ~~CG-4As~~ can carry over ~~4,000 pounds,~~ more than ~~600 pounds~~ beyond its weight! Understand, I love ~~soaring~~, it's the landing of this ~~motorless craft~~ that is so nerve-wracking, especially when there are fierce headwinds.

Even as a ~~pilot~~, I am expected to become an ~~infantryman~~ upon landing. I feel quite satisfied to at last go on a mission to help our country fight this ~~horrendous war.~~

Hope you are well and I miss you very much. Please continue to write to the APO address and maybe a letter will find me. You may not hear from me for a while since we are heading off to ~~Sicily~~, but try not to worry.

Love as always, Fred

The letter shook in my hand. I put it up to the light in the housemaster's room, struggling to read the blacked-out parts. Inside a circle on the letter was the censor's stamp. Where was Fred stationed? It was maddening, trying to read the letter. My imagination got the better of me when I tried to figure it out, making me fear for my husband's life.

I felt depressed when I walked back to the room and became lost in thought about my husband. Madeleine was writing at the desk and asked me about the envelope I was holding.

"It's from my husband." I shoved it deep into my pocket.

"How's he doing? Where's he stationed now?" she asked in her usual inquisitive style.

I pushed it further into my pocket. "It doesn't say."

"Oh, indeed, we aren't supposed to divulge any personal information, anyway." Madeleine buried her head in one of her many books.

I worked hard at all my classes, but never did return to any of the parachute training. I noticed that Madeleine didn't, either. I was determined to succeed in all my other assignments to overcompensate for missing the parachute jumps.

The last few weeks of the wireless transmitting class were a bustling beehive of activity. Everyone was memorizing codes and improving their speeds. I was quite pleased that I consistently exceeded the minimum requirements.

We learned that the aerials for the transmitters were 70 feet long and had to be strung up in attics or disguised as washing lines. I also learned that on a mission I might have to carry a wireless transmitter, weighing 30-40 pounds and camouflaged in a suitcase, for many miles.

I went to the exercise room to build up my muscles. Afterwards, I was thoroughly fatigued and I crawled into bed. I drifted off to sleep, dreaming about being in enemy-occupied France. I thought I heard the door open. Startled, I jumped out of bed. After flipping on the light, I found a strange man lying drunk on the floor.

"*Au, mon Dieu!*" I screamed.

Madeleine got up fast and pulled, then pushed him out of the door into the hall.

"*Merci,*" I said, while standing dumbly in my nightgown. I was impressed by how fast Madeleine acted in emergency situations.

The next day at breakfast, I thought about the previous night and how efficient Madeleine had been in dealing with the drunken man. She was a "strange duck" (like the British said) because she didn't follow all the SOE rules, but was truly dedicated to the cause.

On my last week of training I got a letter from Harry.

> *Dear Sis:*
>
> *My ~~training~~ is now complete. I was sorry to leave "paradise," but I know that I am needed to help win this war. ~~Burma~~ is nothing like the mild climate of the island I left behind. ~~Santa Catalina~~ was an ideal training ground with its hills, steep canyons, along with living among wild goats, buffalo, and ranch cattle. Its rugged coast has numerous coves and beaches, allowing for all kinds of field exercises. But, being on the island did nothing to prepare us for real ~~jungle~~ life. We have been dropped behind ~~Japanese~~ lines to ambush and ~~blow up bridges~~, cut ~~communications~~ and generally harass the ~~Japs~~. I am in charge of the ~~Nisei~~ that I trained on ~~Santa Catalina Island~~. They are a tenacious group of people vigilantly trying to prove how ~~American~~ they are.*
>
> *The way we have been able to survive the ~~Japanese occupation~~ here is with the aid of the ~~native~~ ~~Kachin~~ people, who live in the ~~jungles and hills~~. There are about 200 ~~Kachins~~, who are ~~fierce warriors~~ and hate the ~~Japanese~~ for trying to steal their land.*
>
> *These ~~local guerilla fighters~~ have taught us how to survive in their environment, and in turn we teach them how to ~~fight the Japs~~. Together, the ~~Americans, Nisei,~~ and the ~~Kachins~~ are trying to make a strong, aggressive fighting force.*

After we were ~~defeated~~ in ~~Burma~~ by ~~Japan~~, we had to ~~retreat~~ into an impenetrable, ungodly humid ~~jungle~~ in ~~India.~~ Its ~~monsoon rains~~ bring malaria, cholera, with the plague and typhus a constant threat. Our food is running low and the black ~~swamp~~ buzzes with mosquitoes. Everything smells like ~~elephant dung~~. As we move along we keep sinking as the ~~leeches feed~~ on us. The ~~cane tears~~ at our ~~arms and faces~~ when we attempt to get across the ~~jungle~~. I've been trying to write this letter off and on and it will be a while before it gets posted.

I think of you often and wonder how your "~~WAAC~~ training" is coming along. Please, Sis, try to be safe and careful on your future assignments.

Love, your brother Harry

I reread the letter twice. It had a distinctive, mildewy smell and was full of dirty smudge spots. I held it up to the light and tried to read the blacked-out parts, but to no avail. It was very typical of my brother to be worrying about me going on a mission instead of his own safety. I could only guess what he was doing. I tried to fill in the blanks, and it left me feeling terrified.

Chapter 28
Interrogation

T he final classes at Beaulieu were intense and rough. Every day was filled with activity without a minute's rest. When we weren't running or crawling, more and more information was poured into us. Obviously, six weeks was not enough training, but there was a war going on, and we were needed to sabotage the enemy as soon as possible.

We were taught how to blow up bridges and trains, which would strain the enemy's resources of manpower and supplies. The instructor called it "subversion."

In another class, the trainees learned how to make invisible inks in order to pass messages. The list of things that could make invisible inks included lemon, fruit juices, urine, the white of an egg, onion juice, sugar solution, borax, baking powder, starch, porridge fluid, and even blood. The messages could be discreetly written on cigarette packs and sandwich wrappings, then exposed with the use of a gentle heat.

We were sent into the nearby town to practice shaking off someone shadowing us. We used reflections in shop windows to check to see if we were being followed. The final test consisted of making contact with an unknown person at a prearranged spot, usually a department store or cinema. It was important to learn how to make last-minute boardings of public transport and taxis, all the while making frequent changes in appearance.

One of the last disguise classes taught visual and auditory signals we could use to connect with a contact without anyone suspecting. Some of the signals consisted of puffing on a cigarette a certain way, drumming fingers on a tabletop, squinting with one eye, pretending to have a nervous tic, or a sequence of hand or foot movements. Additional visual signals were behaviors like dropping a newspaper into a waste bin, sticking a message under a bench seat with chewing gum, or throwing down an empty cigarette pack. Any of these secret gestures could be used to identify oneself, and establish clandestine contact with other agents. Verbal messages had to be brief, such as "I'm being followed," or "I've made the drop." The use of drops was essential for leaving messages for others to collect. Various places to leave messages were called "Dead Letter Boxes," and could be a cavity in a wall or tree, a litter bin, or even a piece of furniture.

In the classroom, the teacher, Paul, instructed us in silent and covert lines of approach and return. We were taught that it was best to use lawns and grassy borders, and avoid gravel, flowerbeds, dust, dirt, and mud because of tracking in evidence. We were told to bring poisoned meat in case there were any dogs present. I kept picturing myself in Paris on a real mission, performing all of these tricks of the trade.

The class was instructed about old houses that had ill-fitted sash windows. Because the glass was puttied in, the putty could be cut out to remove the glass. If that didn't work, one could stick treacle to the glass, tap it with a hammer or an elbow, and peel off the shards of glass that stuck to the candy. You would then put your hand through the opening to open the catch or lock. For an assignment, we went on break-in exercises at The Rings or The House in the Woods. We had to break into the house, find a particular room, then get into a specific filing cabinet. To prove that our "mission" was successful, we had to produce evidence of a specific document, then go to an assigned spot and transmit all the information on the document back to the Morse code professor within 20 minutes.

A professional bank robber from Glasgow had been released early from jail and recruited as an instructor. He showed us how to blow safes and schooled us in the skills of lock picking. Locks on old houses were simple locks, easy to force open with a crudely made key or a piece of piano wire. The teacher had us practice on stripped-down door locks, which allowed us to view the internal mechanisms as we worked.

During the very last class for disguises, instructor Paul emphasized that sex was a powerful motivational tool, and could be used to get the enemy to reveal more than they should. He told us that flattery was the key. He informed us that when all else failed, there was always blackmail, which produced fear of exposure of the enemy's private life and weaknesses.

I was sound asleep in my bunk when the door burst open. I jerked up when the light came on to find an officer in a German Abwehr uniform inside our room. If I hadn't had the Resistance to Interrogation class, I might have screamed. Madeleine rolled over and went back to sleep.

"Come with me," he commanded.

I walked to the closet to throw clothes on over my nightgown, but the officer grabbed my arm, shouting, "Now!"

The so-called "officer" dragged me down the hallway to the basement. Adrenaline pulsed through me, jolting my sleepy mind. Mercifully, I remembered the Resistance instruction; we were told to keep our wits at all times if ever arrested by the Gestapo. They were not very intelligent people and always pretended to know more than they did. The teacher said they were guessing most of the time, otherwise they would not be interrogating you. He also added that the Germans had a reputation for being ruthless and terrifying, so we should speak in a slow, clear, firm voice and not answer simple questions immediately. We should not try to be clever; we should create an impression of being stupid. Above all, do not express personal affection or interest in anybody, even your family, if they were mentioned in the interrogation.

Down in the shadowy, dank basement, with a bare bulb descending from the ceiling, the officer demanded in French, *"Nom?"*

"Brigitte LeComte." I was glad I remembered to say a French name at this ungodly hour.

"What is your business in France?" He grasped the top of a wooden chair.

"I am in the FANY," I said, continuing in French.

"Speak up! The what?"

"The First Aid Nursing Yeomanry, sir." I looked longingly at the chair.

"Does this mean you are trying to assist your people to resist against the Germans?" His face was in a contorted snarl, and he sported a frightening stare. Quite suddenly, the uniformed man kicked the chair over.

"Mais non!" I answered.

"You have been seen with someone who is a member of the French Resistance. Put your arms straight over your head!"

"I drive an ambulance." I raised my hands up.

His voice boomed, "Your French accent is flawed. You're a secret agent, aren't you?"

"My father is American and my mother is French." My knees quivered.

"Who's the last person you spoke to personally?"

The "officer" nodded out into the dark at a moving shadow. The light bulb hindered my view. A bucket of ice water was thrown at my thin, flowered nightgown. I let out an uncontrollable scream. I quivered and shook. "My sister, Annette."

The interrogator shouted, "You're lying!"

I tried to restrain my shivering and hugged myself as my nightgown dripped.

"Hands up!" His voice got progressively louder. It felt as though time slowed down.

I put my hands up with my elbows at my side.

He screamed, "Arms over your head, now! What are you doing in Paris?"

My arms went up straight; my teeth chattered. "I'm telling you the truth. I drive an ambulance for the wounded."

After 15 minutes of constant questions thrown at me, my arms began to ache. I tapped a foot to keep myself warm.

"Très bien, Kitty. You're free to go now."

Out of the dark, one of the men came and threw a blanket at me. I picked it up off the floor, wrapped it around my soaked body, and scrambled back to my room.

When I got back to the bedroom, Madeleine was sitting up in bed reading a book. "How did you do, Kitty? I was worried about you."

I grasped the blanket around me tighter, stuttering, "All-all right, I guess."

"The main so-called interrogator that the camp hired used to be a barrister. I know for a fact that they use policemen and ex-policemen who volunteer to come in for these exercises."

"No wonder he was so skilled at cross-questioning me. They threw ice water at me, as you can see." I sniffled, blinking back tears.

"Count your lucky stars that they didn't strip you and make you stand naked for hours under bright lights, like they do with the male trainees. Did they make you stand with books on your head?"

"Non," I whispered.

"Did you stick with your cover story?"

"Oui."

"I'm sure you did just fine, Kitty."

"I'm going to try to go back to sleep, now. *Bonne nuit,* Madeleine." I slipped a dry gown on and held my body tightly in bed.

Chapter 29
Missing

"I'm afraid you got a telegram. It was put under the door while we were out."

I could tell by Madeleine's sympathetic brown eyes that it was bad news. I grabbed it from her and read the short telegram:

> *I regret to inform you that your brother, Harold Arnold Carlson, is missing in action since 20 August, 1943. If further details or other information of his status are received, you will be promptly notified.*
>
> *The Adjutant General*

"*Au, mon Dieu!* Lost in that godforsaken jungle! He must be dead!" I threw myself down on the bunk and sobbed into my pillow.

Madeleine rubbed my back, saying to me in her trance-like way, "They'll find him, they'll find him…"

I stayed in bed the next day while Madeleine went off to class. Doubt rained upon me like a sudden summer storm. What was I doing there? My mind drifted to my weekend on Santa Catalina Island with

Harry. I longed to go back to that paradise and be with my brother, to swim and dance with him again. Every memory brought tears flowing into my pillow. My instincts told me my brother was gone. The last letter from my husband was also disconcerting. Now Fred was an infantryman and not a pilot, like I had been led to believe. *If I lose my husband, I will have no one...*

With half the day gone, I rose from my soaked pillow and washed my face with warm water over and over again in the room's small sink. Did I even have the same character my husband and brother did to be able to successfully complete a mission and contribute to the war effort? They both had a determined patriotism to win this nasty war, which seemed to be getting worse.

I got dressed, hoping a meal would straighten out my throbbing headache.

After dinner I decided to go to the last survival class, which met at night in total darkness. Among a cacophony of insect sounds and strange, unidentifiable animal noises, we were taught how to avoid falling into hidden ponds and bogs. Then we practiced how to move silently through hilltops of brushwood.

We each had to catch and skin a rabbit. I didn't recall ever having seen a rabbit before. They were so adorable. I was able to grab one in the dark because its eyes shone in the night. I couldn't help stroking its soft, fluffy fur. I knew I had to do the dirty deed after I heard the captain shouting for everyone to hurry up and bring the "dinner." I held the helpless creature down with one hand, then squeezed my eyes shut, and with my heavy rock struck the life out of it.

Most of the gals spoke about it when we huddled by the cooking fire. We all were squeamish about killing the bunnies and found it difficult to do.

Madeleine was reading a letter at the desk when I came back from class. "Are you feeling better? I see you went to class."

"*Oui*, I'm glad I did."

"I received a letter from Jacqueline. Let me read it to you."

> *Dear Princesse:*
>
> *Greetings from Ringway Airfield, Manchester. I am enjoying the five-day training here. After jumping from a loft in the hangar by cable, we learned to jump from a barrage balloon at a height of about 900 feet.*
>
> *The next day we were packed into Army jeeps. Most of the girls put on lipstick and make-up right before boarding the Halifax Bomber to impress all the men. At last we got to parachute from a real airplane. The instructor had the girls jump out first so the men would save face and not hold back.*
>
> *There is a flashing red light beside the open drop chute. This one gal, Suzette, kept reaching into her jumpsuit for a flask of brandy. Between sips she kept asking, "When will it turn green?" Every flight thereafter, she refused to jump unless the pilot let her take a few swigs from her hidden flask. We started calling her the "brandy jumper."*
>
> *When it was my turn, after the door opened, I dropped through space, wondering all the while whether the parachute would open and if I would land safely. I pulled the static line (which is a cable attached to the parachute)—this way the chute opens automatically to avoid nervous fumbling.*
>
> *We are required to jump five times in order to complete our training. One of the jumps was at night and another with equipment strapped to our leg. We wear huge, baggy jumping suits with spacious pockets where daggers, rations, flashlights, first aid equipment, wireless parts, and secret maps and papers*

can all be dropped in behind enemy lines. The jackknife is used in case the parachute rigging gets snagged.

Our final jump consisted of pushing a six-foot-long metal container packed with essential supplies out of the chute. Upon landing, we buried our parachutes with a folding shovel that's strapped to our jumpsuit. Then, we had to remove the supplies from the huge containers. We have to unpack fast, which is quite a chore. Typical items for the Resistance are weapons, ammunition, hand grenades, mortar, printing presses, typewriters, miniature cameras and film, folding bicycles, medical kits, fishing tackle, food supplies, wireless receivers and transmitters, wireless crystals, hand generators, clothes with French labels, and packs of cigarettes to be used to sell on the black market to purchase information or convert into currency.

The container has to then be buried or hauled to a nearby river or lake and dumped. This is no easy task since it takes six men or several girls if there are not enough men to move the heavy metal containers. They weigh almost 90 kilos.

One trainee sprained her ankle. It swelled so much that she had to cancel all further jumps. Our ankles are strapped with bandages for support and we wear stout boots with rubber soles to cushion a landing to try and prevent injury.

I'm feeling more confident about the parachute deploying and enjoy the free-fall before it opens. I have successfully completed my five jumps and I'm off to London now to meet with Miss Vivian Armstrong, who will assign me to a mission. Of course, I am hoping it will be in occupied France. Since my husband was killed in battle, I will do anything to help free France. Every time I jump, my mind wanders, and I feel closer to my husband in the heavens above.

Wish me luck, Jacqueline

Jacqueline's letter had a profound effect on me during my last days at Beaulieu. I maintained a determined attitude and managed to pass all my courses. If a widow with a small child could go on a dangerous mission, why couldn't I?

Chapter 30
Officer
Vivian Armstrong

I kept replaying the telegram about Harry in my mind during the two-hour train ride to London, where I was going for an interview. I tried to distract myself by looking out the window at the trees blowing gently in the fall breeze. When the train came closer to the city, I assured myself that the word "missing" did not mean dead.

I was picked up at the station and dropped off at a flat in Orchard Court, off Baker Street in London's West End. There were piles of rubble everywhere from past bombings. An entire row of houses was missing. The butcher shop had a sign on it: *No Meat Today*. The disarray of London reminded me of one of the reasons I joined the SOE in the first place.

A doorman wearing a dark suit and tie led me to the lift that went up to the second floor. He showed me the bathroom, which he strangely called the "waiting room." I sat on the side of the black bathtub, which was surrounded by black and white tiles, deep in thought.

A half hour later a tall, trim woman in her mid-30s, wearing a tweed suit, proffered a hand and introduced herself as Miss Vivian Armstrong, SOE officer. I followed her to an office where she indicated for me to sit on a chair in front of her desk. The walls were covered from ceiling to floor with maps.

Miss Armstrong shuffled some papers and secured a few loose strands of her fair hair with a clip. She was quite pretty, and had an elegant, distinguished look. Madeleine had told me that she also graduated from the Sorbonne.

"I see that you have passed most of your classes at Beaulieu. Let's see here…Weapons Training, Survival, Judo, Interrogation, and Disguise." She said this in her refined British accent.

The officer watched my reaction.

"Mrs. Dwyer, I would like to send you on a mission to Washington, D.C." She tapped my file.

"Washington? The States? Isn't my French good enough?"

"Yes, unless you'd rather parachute into France?"

My face flushed, realizing the reality of the situation as I reflected on my jump tower experience. My hands clenched together.

"I see here that your speed in wireless transmitting is above average. But before you accept this mission, I need to read you a report about your brother."

My eyes widened when she read the telegram out loud to me as part of protocol: "Harold Arnold Carlson, Lt. Col. OSS Detachment 101, found in the jungles of India. Cause of death: malaria." Her blue-gray eyes remained on mine while she studied my face.

After a moment of silence I began to shake. "I knew it! I could feel it! When I received the first telegram, I knew he was gone."

Officer Armstrong rose, came behind my chair, and placed her arm around my shoulder. I was unable to cry, and could only make a slight shuddering noise while shaking. She reached into her suit pocket, retrieved a lace hankie, placed it on my lap, and sat down behind her desk. Miss Armstrong reached across the desk to hold my tightly curled fingers, and waited.

My mind ran through events like a fast-forwarded movie. Harry playing my favorite song at the piano; Harry putting a worm on my fishing hook; Harry laughing with our mother; Harry holding me at the ballroom. I broke down, at first with a small cry and then my dam of tears let loose and I sobbed, wiping my nose with Miss Armstrong's hankie. Miss Armstrong again came over to me and cupped her hand around my shoulders until my burst of sadness was over. When I settled down, she returned to her desk and waited.

"I wanted to inform you of your twin brother's death in order to give you the opportunity to change your mind about going on a mission."

I clutched my hands, anger rising within me. "If my brother died for his country, I'm willing to do so, as well." Try as I might, I couldn't control the tears that flowed from my eyes.

Miss Armstrong waited until my crying was at bay. "I was wondering how you would react to this piece of news." Miss Armstrong left the room, got a glass of water, and placed it in front of me while I blew my nose with the hankie.

"I need you to be sure, Kitty, that you want to serve your country. Perhaps you would like to take some time off?"

"No, I'm sure. I need to feel useful and do want an assignment." My mind wandered over the conversation that Jacqueline had with Madeleine about the death of her own husband. Her determination to fight the war was a virtue to be admired.

"Very well then, you will stay in a small rental house in Washington." Miss Armstrong paused, observing every move I made. "The SOE needs you to obtain French Naval ciphers from a certain ambassador at the Vichy Embassy in Washington, D.C. We will send you undercover as a journalist. If you complete this mission, perhaps then we will use you in France. Because you are an American citizen, you are very suited for this assignment. Are you still interested?"

I hesitated and took a moment to picture myself in Washington. It did sound like a valuable mission. "What about my husband? Do you know if he's been killed?"

"I know where he is in combat, but I have received no information about his status at this time."

I coughed. "I'm sure if he were dead I would have been notified." My lips tightened. I stared at Miss Armstrong, who did not respond. I attempted to regain my composure and said, "I'll take the assignment."

"There will be a small service pay held for you here, but you wouldn't want to do this for the monetary reward. Kitty, you must be 100-percent sure, because if you accept the mission and don't complete it, you will be automatically sent to the Cooler."

I reflected for a moment, remembering the description of the Cooler in Scotland. I sure didn't want to sit out the war there. "I want to be of assistance in any way to serve the SOE and help win this war. After all, my mother was French."

"The SOE is concerned about the French fleet in the Mediterranean. The possession of the ciphers at the embassy in Washington would give us information about what the fleet's intended movements are. We are concerned that the Germans will eventually seize them to help win the war." Miss Armstrong again waited for my response.

"I haven't changed my mind." I gripped the lip of her desk.

"All right then, fill out these papers, update your next of kin and bank details. Come back here at 7:00 a.m. tomorrow. Before you sail out in the morning, I will need to see all of your belongings. You will have to leave all your personal effects with me before you go. This includes all photographs, club membership cards, and any European clothes. Make sure you do not bring anything that would identify you as ever being in England. Do you have a will?"

"A will? No…" I caught my breath.

"I suppose you don't need one, since you only have your husband listed as family now."

Officer Armstrong rose, pushed in her chair, and extended her hand. "See you first thing in the morning, Kitty."

I shook her hand, placed her wet hankie on the desk, and left.

When I got back to my room in Beaulieu, Madeleine's side of the room was bare. I lay on my bunk and cried for my brother, and then felt sad that I didn't get to say goodbye to my friend. We had become quite close during our training on this beautiful estate.

In the morning, I was given a ride back to Orchard Street by the same man who first brought me to Beaulieu a month earlier. One month felt like a lifetime for me now. He chatted away about the weather and scenery, but I felt exhausted and only nodded once in a while.

The doorman gave me a chipper greeting. I rushed past him to go up to Miss Armstrong's office.

"Good morning. I see that you have not changed your mind."

I placed a few photographs on her desk, an assortment of jewelry from my mom, and my wedding band. I felt my ring finger. The indentation from my wedding ring had now disappeared.

Miss Armstrong placed everything in a box with a lid, then labeled it with my real name. A dark emptiness enveloped me when I parted with my personal effects. I felt an eerie, death-like feeling, but then reminded myself that I was only going to Washington.

She went through my suitcase and all the pockets of the clothes, inspecting the labels. Officer Armstrong checked the clothes I was wearing. I had to take off my shoes for inspection.

Officer Armstrong finished going through my handbag. "I need you to sign the Official Secrets Act."

After I signed it, she handed me a piece of stationery.

"Now, write a letter to your husband. Make it light and chatty, such as, 'all is well and keeping busy in the Army.' I will make sure he gets it. Please do not mention your brother's death and keep your cover as a WAAC."

Miss Armstrong lit a cigarette and buried herself in a stack of papers, which gave me some privacy to gather my thoughts to write to my husband. After formulating my thoughts, I placed the letter on the desk.

"Here's your boat ticket to New York, with train tickets to Washington, D.C." Officer Armstrong placed a small Colt revolver and bullets on the desk. "Keep this in your handbag on you at all times. Here are some pills." She put an assortment of different colored tablets on her desk in front of me. "This yellow pill will induce sleep for six hours and can be administered easily in an enemy's tea. Here's a pill that produces stomach disorders—handy against the enemy. This is Benzedrine, a stimulant, if you need to stay awake to complete a mission. Now, here is the L pill, which is a suicide pill. It contains cyanide. Hide this in the top pocket inside your jacket. It can also be hidden in a tube of lipstick. If taken, death will occur within 15 seconds, but remember it must be bitten, not swallowed, to work. The L pill should only be used in extreme circumstances, such as during interrogation to avoid disclosing clandestine information or if obvious inevitable torture might occur."

Miss Armstrong studied my eyes and waited for any reaction.

I tried very hard to keep a blank face.

"Kitty, if you have any doubts about this mission or feel that you are not the type to complete it successfully, it's not too late to say no. You can leave without any embarrassment. The SOE needs to be sure of your intentions."

"You can rely on me."

Chapter 31
Mission
Washington, DC

The ship ride to the United States was what my perplexed soul needed. I was glad to be confined to my berth because of crossing dangerous waters with the possibility of enemy attack. The long journey clarified my resolve to serve my country. I felt a bit unsure about my brother's death, being unable to see his body, but in my heart I knew he was gone. I spent as many days as possible breathing in the salty air, attempting to soothe the grief within me. I wrote in a notebook, spilling out all my anguish like it was a close friend, even though I knew I would have to destroy it.

Upon reaching the United States, I had a few passing thoughts about skipping the entire mission and going home, but in reality I had nothing to do in New York except wait for Fred to come home.

Several trains later, I was met by an Army private who drove me to a rental house in Georgetown. I almost said, *"Bonjour,"* but covered it up with a hello. He didn't say much, and dropped me off after handing me the key and my two suitcases.

The elegant house on O Street in Washington, a suburb of Georgetown, had been used by the British embassy to house temporary members of its staff. The narrow street was shaded and a few blocks from the picturesque Potomac River. I put the key in the door and entered the gracious home, which had high ceilings and well-polished wooden floors. I unpacked my small amount of clothes, putting them into a dark walnut dresser. My notebook was on top. I ripped it up, remembering that diaries were forbidden. In the large closet, I was happy to see party dresses and many pairs of high-heeled shoes.

I opened up my wireless transmitter and strung out the aerial into a tree from a window in the bedroom that faced a back alley. I transmitted to Miss Armstrong my arrival. A brief time later, I received a message back telling me to go to a dinner party the next night in uptown Washington on Wyoming Avenue, with instructions to sit next to a Monsieur Lavinfosse, a French Naval attaché. I pushed my suitcase radio deep underneath my bed, then put on my nightgown, hoping for a good night's sleep.

All of a sudden, I heard a knock on the door. I grabbed the .32 Colt that Miss Armstrong had issued me, threw a coat on, and put the weapon in my pocket.

"Who's there?" I attempted to use a strong voice.

A man in work clothes barged in carrying a large, pump-like device. "I'm the exterminator."

I panicked, chastising myself for not locking the door. I felt the metal weapon in the pocket of my coat.

He closed the door and spoke in a low voice, "I'm from the OSS. I have to check your house for bugs."

The rapid beat of my heart subsided. He methodically searched floorboards, phone outlets, even under wall panels. I managed to blurt out a "thank you" when he left without a word.

That Saturday afternoon I tried on two of the dresses that were my size. I twirled in each one and chose the long, sweeping, formal dress—

the fanciest one in the closet. The light aqua accentuated my eye color. It had a stunning gilt-threaded embroidered waist with a full pleated skirt. The deep V-neck accommodated my large breasts, but did show a bit too much cleavage for my comfort. It had been quite a while since I'd had the pleasure of dressing up. Much to my delight, there was a pair of silk stockings on the top shelf of the closet. I slipped them on after retrieving a girdle from my underclothes, then tried on a nice pair of heels. The marvelous reflection in the mirror gave me the confidence I now needed.

"Why, darling," I said in French, imitating my mother's voice, "you look poised as well as beautiful."

I was grateful that she had instilled in me a feel for style and a sense of adventure. How very lucky I felt. With my lipstick applied with precision, I looked forward to the mission ahead.

Many hours later, the same Army private who had transported me from the train knocked on my door and drove me to the party. He introduced himself to the hostess, and in a whisper asked her to seat me next to the Vichy ambassador. Then he left, saying he would pick me up later.

The hostess, a fine-looking woman, seated me next to a stout, middle-aged man in a uniform. He rose and introduced himself. "Monsieur Lavinfosse. Happy to make your acquaintance." He kissed my hand with enthusiasm.

"Elizabeth Thorton."

"Shall I pour you a glass of wine?"

"I would love some, thank you. What a nice collection of medals on your uniform. Do you work here in Washington?" I flashed him a few times with my eyelashes.

"I'm a Naval attaché at the Vichy Embassy. And what brings you to this fine city?"

"I work as a journalist."

"Are you new to the area?"

"Yes, I've been here a few days. I'm from New York." I pulled at my neckline.

"I'd love to show you around this beautiful city. It is magnificent in the fall. Most people enjoy Washington more in the spring during the cherry blossom time, but I prefer the crisp air of this season."

The waiters brought the main meal.

I took a bite of the roast beef. "What an elegant dinner."

"We are fortunate to enjoy all this food without having to deal with ration coupons. Tell me, Elizabeth, do you live here in Washington with your husband?" One eyebrow rose in question.

"My husband and I have had differences and are separated. This is why I'm keeping busy working. And tell me, Ambassador, are you married?" I leaned in closer.

"My wife's on holiday with my children. She's American, like you, but not as attractive. May I pour you more wine?"

"Yes, thank you." My eyes were locked to his as if drawn by a magnet.

We continued chatting while enjoying the large meal. After dessert I slipped the ambassador a piece of paper with my street address on it. "Call on me sometime…soon," I said in a low voice.

Monsieur Lavinfosse jumped at the chance. "I'd be happy to give you a tour of the city on Monday."

"Can you come by in the evening? I work during the day."

"Certainly. I'll bring a bottle of fine European wine that you will adore."

Upon seeing my escort arrive, I got up from my seat. Monsieur Lavinfosse stood up to say goodbye. I was quite stunned by how short he was.

After getting back to my room, I transmitted a message to Miss Armstrong.

Met with Ambassador, making progress, will report back on Tuesday, Kitty

Monday, after a light dinner, I dressed with care, and put on a few drops of ordinary perfume I bought from a store in town. I wistfully remembered Miss Armstrong placing my last precious bottle of *Guerlain* from my mother in the storage box before I left. It was my favorite, but I knew that having French perfume would be too suspicious in the States.

A knock came at the door at 7:00 p.m., and I was ready. I knew I could play the part because I had acted in a variety of theatrical productions in college.

"Mrs. Thorton, so very nice to see you again." The ambassador kissed my hand and handed me a bottle of wine.

"Please, Monsieur Lavinfosse, call me Elizabeth." The ambassador's height bothered me again, and I was anxious to seat him to equal our heights a little better. I sat on the couch and patted a spot next to me.

We sat close together.

"Please call me Henri. Elizabeth, my dear, what is the name of the perfume you are wearing? It smells delicious."

"Oh, it's nothing special. I'm afraid I've used up all of my mother's perfume, *Guerlain.*"

His eyes twinkled. "Your mother's French?"

"Yes, but she passed away earlier this year."

"I'm so sorry. *Parlez-vous Français?*"

"*Mais oui.* I graduated from the Sorbonne University." I put my hand on his lap. "Henri, *s'il vous plaît*, tell me all about your job at the embassy. I'm sure it's of great importance." I spoke to him in his native language while adjusting the bodice on my dress ever so slightly.

The ambassador's eyes stayed on my breasts and he enjoyed speaking with me in rapid French. "I was the director of Naval Intelligence at the Ministry in France, then was transferred to the United States as a Naval attaché. What about your husband, Elizabeth? What does he do?"

"My husband is in the Army overseas. I'm ashamed to say our marriage has failed, due to never having been able to produce any children, but he's Catholic and will not give me a divorce." My eyes averted downward; I fussed with my dress. I rubbed one of my eyelids, hoping Monsieur Lavinfosse would think it was a tear.

179

Henri sympathetically took my hand in his. "My marriage also is a failure, and my wife and I are very distant with each other."

He leaned in, kissing my cheek. In return, I kissed his lips. We enjoyed a long, amorous kiss. I was surprised at how stimulating it was.

We continued embracing until I forced myself to pull away. "I'd love to try your French wine."

To cool the passion I felt heating up within Henri and myself, I went into the kitchen to find a bottle opener. I returned to the living room and placed it next to the wine, then went back to get two glasses. I felt Henri's eyes on my legs and fixed the seam on my stockings.

With the glasses next to the wine, Henri opened the bottle with a quick move of the corkscrew. We both laughed when it made a cheerful popping sound. After pouring the wine, he raised his glass and I raised mine for a toast.

"To France and America, may we become close friends."

I sat farther away from him this time while we enjoyed our wine.

"I'm afraid I must retire early for work tomorrow." I crossed my slim, silk-clad legs.

"Can I see you again, Elizabeth?" His gaze focused on my breasts.

"I would enjoy that. It's hard to be all alone in this city." I wrote my phone number down and handed it to him. "Please, Henri, call me soon."

He kissed my hand gently and took the paper. "I have enjoyed your company. It has been a while since I've been with such a beautiful woman."

Chapter 32
The French Ambassador

Monsieur Lavinfosse called me the next night, wanting to come over. I put him off until a few days later. I wandered around the city and enjoyed the fall colors displaying themselves on the maple trees. The bursting multi-shades of yellows and reds on the sugar maples gave my eyes a delightful treat.

As I walked around a nearby park, I thought about the art of seduction, which certainly was a better method of obtaining information than killing or torture. The surprise interrogation I experienced at Beaulieu was not a method I wanted to duplicate to obtain the Vichy ciphers. I strolled along the Potomac, wistfully thinking of my husband so far away. Henri Lavinfosse was twice my age and it took all my will to want to seduce him, even though I had enjoyed the intimacy of the other night. I had to go slow and remain cool, throwing out little tidbits of myself like pieces of bread for fish in a pond.

I dipped my hand in the cool water of the river and felt someone nearby. I thought I saw someone Henri's size behind a tree, and decided to take a different route back to the house.

The following week, Henri brought me a large, beautiful bouquet of roses, declaring in French, "I missed you so much."

My face flushed into a pink hue. I breathed in the luscious fragrance of the red roses and bent over, thanking him with a long kiss. This time I suggested we go for a walk to avoid the inevitable possibility of ending up in bed.

"Washington is quite lovely this time of year, even though you missed the cherry blossoms. How's your work coming along?" Henri inquired.

"Fine," I answered, wanting to keep away from the subject of myself. "How's your job? It must be a difficult one, given the status of the war." I looped my arm through his.

"How right you are. I do love America, as well as France, and I am worried about the Germans." He looked deeply into my eyes.

When we got back to my house, Henri reached to open the door.

"I am not feeling very well. Let's get together next week. I will cook you a special dinner," I said.

"Of course. I will bring the wine, *ma chérie.*"

"*Bonsoir*, Henri."

"*Bonsoir*, my little butterfly."

I shut the door and a mischievous smile spread upon my face. I reached under my bed for my transmitter and sent a report to Miss Armstrong.

Making progress with H.L.

I waited a half hour and received a transmission back from her:

Happy with your answer but please speed mission up. When complete, visit friends at Apartment 715B Wardman Park Hotel.

With great care, I prepared a dinner of roasted chicken, potatoes, green beans, and a special dessert to complement it. I hoped the seductive meal would be to Henri's liking. This time he brought two bottles of wine, making me suspect he wanted to ply me with alcohol in order to have me succumb to his desires. It worked. With most of the wine consumed, my guard was completely gone, and we stumbled toward the bedroom.

On the edge of the bed, Henri lavished me with tiny kisses up and down my neck and into my breasts. He undressed me as I slipped under his spell and eagerly tore off his clothes. Henri, with gentle compassion, explored every part of my body, transporting me into a world that I never dreamed would be possible to enter. His lovemaking was ever so tender, interspersed with romantic French intimacies. We became one as "Oh…" escaped from my lips when his climax followed mine. I lay in a stunned stupor. Henri continued to tenderly stroke my arm even after his passion was spent.

Afterward, we lay in bed sharing his cigarette. He whispered in French, *"Merci, mon amour,* you have satiated me and fulfilled a need that has been void way too long. You see, I did not marry for love, but for suitability."

I was unable to respond, to reveal my identical feelings. I lost myself in his arms, deep in thought about my infidelity and my new emotions. Henri held me. I was torn between wanting him again, to feel that heavenly sensation once more, but guilt came upon me.

I forced myself to turn away from his amorous touch. "Henri, you must go now. I get up much too early and need to be to work on time."

"I will leave if you allow me to come back tomorrow night. I cannot wait an entire week after savoring you for the first time.'"

I nodded my head into the pillow, avoiding his luscious, melting eyes as he got up, dressed, and left.

As soon as Henri was gone, I transmitted a report back to the home base.

Will be obtaining important information tomorrow night, K

I tossed and turned most of the night, and then I drifted off, dreaming that Henri slapped my face after I asked him for the ciphers and then called me a spy. Upon waking in a sweat, I wondered if my timing would be right.

I spent the next morning in constant thought about my relationship with Fred. Henri was nowhere near as handsome as my husband, but he was far more skilled as a lover, and now, for the very first time, I knew what the meaning of orgasm was.

I went through the dresses in the closet, and reflected on my training. I did want to be successful in this important mission. The SOE did not train women in the art of seduction for the purposes of espionage, but they alluded to it many times with the philosophy of "all's fair in love and war." Paul, the disguise instructor, had touched upon the subject frequently. My greatest asset was to use my feminine charms. Now that we were on intimate terms, I was certain I could get what I wanted from Henri. My role was to pretend, and to hide my real feelings at all times, which I found was not an easy task after I had exposed myself physically.

That night Henri brought from his pocket a dainty box with a thin lace bow, thus building my confidence that I was getting closer to my goal.

"*Pour toi,* my darling."

I untied the delicate bow and forced a few tears to well up in my eyes. "Oh, Henri, you are so very thoughtful. It's my favorite." It was a precious bottle of *Guerlain.* I refrained from opening it to release the heavenly fragrance.

"You deserve the best, *ma chérie.* Now every time you wear it you will think of me." He held my hand, kissing me hungrily, wanting more.

I moved away, and placed the unopened box on the small table next to the couch. I was overcome by memories of my mother, but forced myself to stay on task. "*Mon chéri,* if you wish to give me a special gift, I need something more important that will enhance my new career; especially since my marriage may not last." I gave him a passionate kiss, then broke away, leaned over, and tilted the perfume box.

"What is it that you need, my little butterfly?"

"I have a friend at the Office of Naval Intelligence who needs the French Naval ciphers. He has told me that it would help France to reunite and be free of the German occupation."

Henri remained silent. I took his hand and led him to the bedroom. *Did I move too soon on this?* I worried to myself.

After we had both thoroughly satisfied each other, I kissed his long, pronounced nose, then stroked it with one finger. "Henri, *mon amour*, you told me you did not want your country to fall to the Axis. I know that my friend can help in this situation."

He sighed while fondling my breasts, and delicately kissed each of my nipples. "*Très bien,* the name of the embassy code clerk is Monsieur Benoit. You can get the ciphers from him with money, and I know he is poorly paid." Henri rolled over. His gentle snoring lulled me to sleep.

Once he left in the morning, I transmitted a quick report:

Obtained clerk's name, getting closer.

A half hour later I received a transmission back:

After your visit…go to 715B Wardman Park Hotel… bring gift…May God keep you.

When I made the bed, I noticed Henri had left a substantial amount of money on the nightstand.

Chapter 33
Ciphers

There was one clean dress left for me to wear, but it was not my size. I put it on and tried to cover my exposed bodice with a sweater. I put the money deep inside my brassiere and took the bus to the French Embassy.

There was a plain-looking man at the front desk, who said in French, "May I help you?"

I stumbled on my words and asked in French, "Are, are you Monsieur Benoit?"

"*Oui*, Madame."

I searched past him and saw no one in sight. I reached inside my bodice, fanned out the stack of money, and placed it on the desk. "I need the French cipher books. I promise to keep them for just a few hours."

Benoit scooped up the cash, stuffed it into his jacket pocket, and went into a back room.

I closed my eyes, and prayed for the codebooks and not a gendarme showing up to arrest me.

The clerk reappeared within minutes, handed me two large, dark-colored cipher books, and looked at the clock on the wall. "You must return within two hours."

I snatched the books and put them in my empty suitcase. My heels clicked down the hallway. I took a streetcar to Wardman Park Hotel. In the elevator was a gentleman who inquired what floor I was going to.

"The 10th," I lied.

He kept staring at me. I clutched my case and kept my eyes on the passing elevator numbers. Beads of perspiration were beginning to form on my forehead. He got out on the eighth floor.

The elevator dinged on the 10th floor and I pressed it back down to the seventh, satisfied that he wasn't following me. After knocking the Morse code word "victory" on the door, a man opened it and snatched my suitcase.

There before me was an intense, bustling atmosphere, like a construction zone in New York City with its equipment filling every space. I shrank back into the corner feeling useless, staring at the entire apartment spread with its assortment of photographic lights, cameras, tripods, and cables. Men were rushing all about. The ciphers were photographed, then the Photostats were spread around the room to dry on spare tables, furniture, even on the floor. The room had clouds of cigarette smoke, and several people started coughing until a window was opened to bring in fresh air.

After being handed the dried Photostats, I walked with caution to the courier's address sent to me by Miss Armstrong. I checked my surroundings at all times, like I had learned to do in finishing school. I found the street and hunted for the apartment. I tapped the prearranged Morse code on the door.

"Here is mail from your cousin," I said in a low voice.

Someone opened the door a crack, responding, "Good, I have missed her." He grabbed the folder before I could see his face.

Now I had to return the codebooks.

I walked down the hall to the French Embassy, the handle of my suitcase sticky from my sweaty palm. I made sure my posture was straight in order to express confidence. There were many people at the front desk this time. I glanced nervously toward Monsieur Benoit.

He graciously lied, *"Bonjour*, Sis, you're right on time for lunch." Monsieur Benoit came from behind the desk, put his arm around me and guided me out of the office. Once we got outside he took the suitcase and we parted ways.

Henri rang me up at his usual time and I agreed to have him over.

He lavished me with his French lovemaking techniques and once again I was lost in his charms. As we lay in bed, I told him I was going to New York to meet with my husband, who was on leave and had written to see if we could patch up our marriage. Henri looked like a neglected puppy, so I lied and promised I would be returning in a few weeks. He showered me with kisses, starting at my toes and with leisure worked his way over every part of my body. I swooned, tingling with every touch, losing myself for the very last time.

The next week, I received a transmission from Miss Armstrong:

Received present…Perfect gift for Uncle Sam…Visit me at your convenience…May God keep you.

Chapter 34
A New Mission

"**K**itty, it's so good to see you. How was your ship passage? Was it safe?"

Miss Armstrong gave me a warm embrace.

With surprise, I hugged her back. "It was fine, but I was confined to my compartment due to the possibility of the German U-boats in the seas."

"Your mission was highly successful. The ciphers exposed the Vichy fleet movements. French Prime Minister Pierre Laval had been refusing to send the ships to Martinique for the duration of the war. Britain and America were worried that in time the Germans would seize them. Because you were able to obtain the Vichy ciphers, now we know exactly what Germany's involvement is with the French fleet. I don't know how you did it, Kitty, but you are a courageous woman." Miss Armstrong studied my face. I could see her brain computing my surprise.

"Thank you," tumbled out of my mouth as I pondered the word "courageous."

Officer Armstrong switched to French. "The SOE is very interested in sending you to France. Your ability to complete this mission was of great importance. We now have a shortage of radio operators in the field and it is reaching crisis proportions. You will be sent to work with your former roommate, Madeleine. Are you interested?"

I bit the inside of my cheek. "I'm not sure I am courageous enough to parachute jump into France."

"Oh, don't worry about that. We'll transport you, along with two other agents, by a small Lysander airplane."

"I do want to help out in France. But tell me, Miss Armstrong, have you gotten any more letters from my husband?"

"I have. I'll read you his letter." She slowly went through a file on her desk.

I bounced one of my knees in anticipation. At least, because Officer Armstrong was reading it to me, it was uncensored.

Kathleen, my dearest:

I am assigned to Operation Husky in Sicily; I have a great pal now who will be going on this mission with us. Walter is a war correspondent with United Press. He doesn't want to go, but he told me that he absolutely did not want to lose his job. I can't believe the Army allows these volunteers to go on war missions and endanger their lives. At least I get benefits from the Army, while he is a civilian.

We are to fly to the Italian island of Sicily to gain control of the Mediterranean from the Axis. We are joining the fight with British and Canadian forces. Britain has a shortage of glider pilots and requested our help. I am honored to be selected to fly across the channel.

This will be quite a dangerous mission because the Germans can directly fire at us and we could be blown to smithereens. We have always been told since the beginning, landing a glider is like a planned accident. The pilots never know who will survive it. But then, after all, it is a motorless aircraft.

Try not to worry. We are a brave bunch of soldiers and all want to help to put an end to this war. It is estimated that 1,000 people a day are dying for the cause. We are determined to knock Italy out of the war. Look out Hitler, here we come!

I think of Harry often; I'm sure you do too. I want you to know that I am very proud that you are also serving our country by being in the WAACs. It is comforting to me that you are safe and won't ever be involved in combat.

Love as always, Fred

After finishing the letter from Fred, Miss Armstrong searched my face for a reaction. I tried to keep it blank, but my eyebrows wandered into a worried, knitted expression.

"I have told you before, Kitty, you may choose to pass on this mission. I know you have been through a lot of emotional stress with the death of your brother, and now have the anxiety of your husband overseas, wondering if he will return. I'm sure the Washington mission was not an easy task for you. I will not lie—sending you on this high-risk assignment to France will be putting you in a very dangerous situation. Wireless operators have a life expectancy of six weeks because the Germans have devices to pick up signals. You will be working all alone as a clandestine operator in German-occupied Paris. If you need time to think it over, please do so. It can be easy to be discovered, then interrogated by the Nazis and killed. I must remind you that being a part of the Security Operatives Executive, you are not part of the military and would not have the protection under the international laws of warfare. I will not sugarcoat the mission—you could be shot or imprisoned and may never return." Miss Armstrong paused, her eyes boring into mine.

I tried to speak with conviction, but my voice trembled. "I have a special affinity for France because it was my mother's homeland and I went to college there." I paused, my hands knotted together. "I want to serve my country like my brother did, and as my husband continues to do."

"*Très bien.*" The intelligence officer continued in French, "You may still back out of this, but the SOE would be grateful to have such a skilled agent like yourself." Miss Armstrong displayed a small smile. "Let's make sure your affairs are in order before you leave. Please give me any personal effects you may have accumulated from Washington."

I went through my suitcase, placing the bottle of *Guerlain,* still in the exquisite box the ambassador had given me, on her desk. I took out the pills with hesitation.

"Keep the pills, make sure you have all of them that I gave you from the Washington mission. You may need them in France." Officer Armstrong looked at me, scouting my face for any sign of fear.

I put the pills back in my pocket.

"Now, you'll need to go to the showroom on Margaret Street to be fitted for used French clothing. They will also provide you with French underwear. Can you open your mouth, please?"

I did as I was told, but was curious what she was looking for.

"You will need to have a filling replaced."

After I flinched, she added, "The French only use gold. It's necessary to look completely French if ever stopped or caught by the Nazis. Here's the dentist we use." She handed me a slip of paper. "Your hairstyle will not do, either. It's not French enough." Miss Armstrong placed the address of a salon next to the dentist's information. "After completing these tasks, come back to my office and we'll go over your new cover." The SOE officer watched every move I made while talking to me. "Do you have any questions?"

"Not that I can think of right now," I answered in French, lost in thought.

Chapter 35
Tangmere

The free "shopping spree" was enjoyable, even though the clothes were French peasant types. I got my hair done in a French cut, and proceeded to the dental office last. This procedure was not something I was looking forward to.

After my dental visit, I knocked on Miss Armstrong's door and entered upon hearing her response, *"Entrez."*

She was behind her huge desk surrounded by piles of paperwork and puffing on a cigarette. After I put my bag of clothes down, she reached under her desk and pulled out a battered suitcase.

"Put all your French clothes in here. I have received from the forgery department the latest ration cards and a French identity card for you. Keep them on you at all times when you move about Paris. As your cover, your birthplace in France is located in an obscure district where the town hall has been bombed, making it impossible for any authorities to look up information. Because your French accent has a slight foreign trace, your cover will be that your father was French and your mother was American. Your new name will be Jeanette LeBlanc."

Miss Armstrong exhaled a veil of cigarette smoke that snaked high into the air. "Madeleine will meet your plane. She has been in France helping to set up the Prosper Mission. She'll assist you in getting started. I know you have developed a close relationship with her and you will work together well. I'll bring you to Tangmere tomorrow to wait for the full moon that night to fly into France. You'll have tonight to go over your new identity. Spend the evening in the upstairs apartment. Do you have any questions?"

"*Non.*"

"Kitty," Officer Armstrong reached over the desk and touched my hand. "I cannot emphasize enough that if for any reason whatsoever you feel you cannot go on this mission, let me know now. I can transfer you to a less dangerous job. At this point, it is more shameful to go to occupied Paris and let everyone down. Do you have any further concerns?" She removed her hand, and while waiting for a reply, lit a cigarette, inhaled, and tapped the ash into the overflowing ashtray.

"I have given this mission a lot of thought and I am determined to help the cause and go." I rubbed my eyes, hiding my anxiety.

Officer Armstrong opened her top drawer and handed me a piece of stationary. "In your room, write a letter to your husband, and I will try to get it to him. Keep it light and as cheerful as possible. And remember, he thinks you are a WAAC. Do you have any more concerns?"

"*Non.*"

"Here's the key to your room. By the way, Kitty, you have an excellent command of the French language, which is one of the reasons you have been chosen for this assignment. See you in the morning. Try to have a good night's sleep." Miss Armstrong went back to writing in one of her files.

In the sparse room, I read my new cover over and over, rolling my R's. I liked my new name and made up conversations about my mother and father. Satisfied, I wrote a letter to Fred. I bit the end of the pen and did not enjoy being untruthful to him. At finishing school it was said, "Get used to lying and develop the ability to invent stories. It's the way to be a proper agent."

That night I had a fitful sleep on the narrow, uncomfortable cot in the small room. I dreamed Fred flew his glider plane into Paris, was shot down and hurt. Madeleine picked him up in an ambulance and nursed him back to health. Upon awaking, I reflected on Madeleine, and how much I missed her. I was looking forward to renewing our friendship.

Tangmere was an excellent location for a landing strip to get to

France since it was close to the English Channel. Officer Armstrong and I left London in the afternoon. From there it took a few hours to get to the Sussex coast. The Lysander wouldn't leave until 2100 hours, when the moon was at its highest, giving good visibility for the pilot to land near the woods outside of Paris.

"We're going a bit early for one last hurrah of a jolly, hearty supper before your flight." Miss Armstrong pointed out different sites on the way, attempting to ease my obvious tension.

The driver let us off and I followed Miss Armstrong down a long path. We approached a cottage in Tangmere that was hidden by tall hedges and couldn't be seen from the road. It was covered with profuse ivy, like a plain dress decorated with ruffles of lace. From the outside it was quiet except for an occasional tweeting bird seeking refuge for the evening.

It was an enchanting, 17th-century house with low ceilings and thick walls. Miss Armstrong showed me around on the ground floor where there were two large rooms and a kitchen. One of the living rooms was filled with cigarette smoke, and everyone was chatting in French. There was a mixed collection of chairs, some arranged around a coal fireplace. The second living room was the operations room, and had two long trestle tables. I saw an ordinary telephone, and a green scrambler phone line for confidential conversations, along with an assortment of files and charts. Several people were listening to the BBC French news program. Everyone knew Officer Armstrong and greeted her with warmth.

In the operations room a large map of France covered the wall with red marks showing high-risk areas for flak. There were many RAF pilots milling about, some receiving instructions for various flights.

Miss Armstrong pointed out the field on the map. "This is where you'll be landing. It's about 160 kilometers north-northwest of Angers."

I followed her upstairs, where she showed me a room with three beds. I set my suitcase down and she put another one next to it. "Here's your Mark II wireless transmitter. This one's 30 pounds and will fit well in your two-foot-long French suitcase. We have very few sets available."

She faced me squarely. "I need you to know that during this war, wireless transmitting agents have had the highest casualties of all agents." Officer Armstrong placed a small pistol on the bed. "Keep this on you at all times. Have you memorized your cover?"

"*Mais oui,*" I said, attempting to sound confident.

"I need you to transmit this message to France. It will be received by the BBC French service and announced in the middle of their evening program." Miss Armstrong handed me the paper.

It read: *les marguerites fleuriront ce soir (the daisies will bloom tonight).* I looked at her quizzically.

Officer Armstrong whispered, "This tells the reception committee agents listening to the program to prepare for the arriving Lysander. Supper is at 1950 hours. After you send the message, spend a short time practicing your speed."

After transmitting the message, I practiced typing briefly, making sure I was up to par, then freshened up in the bathroom down the hallway.

I joined the other agents downstairs for the farewell dinner party. The woman at the table on my right introduced herself as Cécile. I, in turn, used my new code name, Jeanette. Her steel-rimmed glasses gave her an old-maidish appearance. When Cécile reached for her glass of wine and took a sip, I glanced at her well-aged, spotted hand. She seemed too old to be an agent, and I thought she must be in her late 40s, which could be why she wasn't parachuting in. Seated on my left was an agent with the code name Diane. She was quite shy, or maybe she was just nervous. She enjoyed smoking more than chatting or eating.

There was obvious tension in the air as we waited for 2100 hours, when the Lysander would fly in. The conversation was kept strictly to mundane topics like the food, weather, and was in the French language.

"Have you looked outside? The full moon is a welcome beacon for our trip," Cécile announced to Diane and me.

I took a piece of bread, rose, and opened the curtain a bit for a quick look, then returned to my seat. Even though it was a warm night, all the windows were kept closed for security. "It's heavenly."

Diane paused between cigarettes and nodded.

A half hour before takeoff, Diane, Cécile, and I got into a large Ford estate car with Miss Armstrong, and an Army driver whisked us off to the airfield.

In the hangar, Miss Armstrong inspected each agent. She checked all the labels on the clothes we were wearing, and searched our pockets. "There must not be any English cigarettes or bus tickets. A small lapse like that could dash weeks of planning." She touched each of us like a protective mother hen securing her chicks around her. Next, she put huge money belts on each of us. "All this money was printed in England and has gone through a dirtying process in order to look well circulated. The stacks of bills have been pinned together through the watermark with large hatpins like the French banks do. Give it all to your mission organizer."

Miss Armstrong secured the L pill inside our blouses, speaking in soft tones with her precise English accent. "Remember, if necessary, bite your cyanide pill. If you were to swallow it whole it would not take effect fast enough."

I noticed that Diane tapped her foot the entire time, and Cécile's hands shook until she clasped them together in front of her French skirt.

Miss Armstrong took each agent aside one by one to listen to our cover stories. She then gave Diane and Cécile each a gold compact for a going away present. "You can always use them in an emergency, like money."

I was the last one to review my cover with her. She nodded in approval as I touched a lovely silver bird pinned on her lapel that reflected brightly in the moonlight. "What a pretty brooch," I said.

She took it off and secured it to my coat.

"I can't take it."

"Oh, but you must. It's perfect for you. A little bird to bring you good luck." She turned away when we heard the Lysander descend.

We all stood on the tarmac, trying to see the small aircraft in the shine of the luminous moon elevated in the sky. The plane had been painted black, or it would have shone like a spotlight. The pilot put out a short ladder, calling to us to climb aboard. We stowed our luggage under the only two wooden seats. I sat on the floor in the tight confines of the airplane.

The RAF pilot introduced himself as John. Once we had our flight helmets on, he showed us how to plug into the intercom. John demonstrated how to switch each microphone on and off. Then he sat at the controls, slid the roof shut, primed the engine, and up we soared.

Chapter 36
Westland Lysander

The pilot tried to ease our anxiety by chatting through his microphone.

"Lizzies move slowly, only 200 miles per hour. They are half the speed of a German fighter aircraft. Because it is a short-winged monoplane, it flies at a much lower altitude, which makes it easier to land in muddy fields and on very small airstrips, like the one we'll be landing on tonight."

I pointed to his dark blue, rolled-neck collar, and said through my microphone, *"Joli* sweater."

"Pilots have to wear French clothing under their uniforms in case they're shot down and then have to blend into the French countryside. I even have an escape kit to carry shoes, a béret, French money, maps, a compass, fishing hook and line, and concentrated food tablets, along with forged identity papers."

"It's good you're prepared," Cécile remarked.

"On last month's mission, I was about to land my Lizzy. I was waiting for the signal, when German soldiers came running out of the woods shouting and firing their rifles. I was able to throttle up and get out of there fast."

This bit of information started Diane's foot to bob. I reached over and patted her hand, as Madeleine would have done.

We all marveled over the excellent visibility of the view from the plane and went across the Channel in the silvery glow of the moonlight. I noticed a flask of whiskey peeking out of the pilot's jacket pocket.

Four hours later, the moon was a magical globe lighting the loops of the Loire River on this beautiful, clear night. We hovered over a wooded area with a field in the distance. John put his right hand on his Colt .45 in its holster, giving me the jitters. I knew we were about to land in enemy territory.

"There's the inverted L of torches. Now we need to wait for the right code letter to flash." Below us were miniature flare paths consisting of three pocket flashlights tied to sticks in the shape of an inverted L. "Ahh, there's our letter, mission almost complete."

The Morse code for the letter Q flashed below.

"Now we can descend." The pilot reached down on his holster, put the safety catch back on his weapon, and landed in what he told us was a sympathetic farmer's field.

A man called Gilbert came on board, shook our hands, and helped us down the ladder. In a hurry, two male agents and one female agent replaced us to head back to London in the plane.

"You are now in the Vallée de la Loire, near Angers," Gilbert said in a local French accent. "I wish to thank you all for aiding the *réseaux*—the Resistance. We are in desperate need of help. Without our radio operators and couriers we are like pigeons without wings."

Out of the woods near the field, a familiar voice called, *"Bonsoir."* I could tell it was Madeleine when the moonlight lit up her face, even though her face was now framed by dyed red hair.

We embraced. She kissed both my cheeks, whispering, "I missed you."

"Tu m'as manqué aussi," I whispered back.

"Call me Marie."

"And I am Jeanette."

Gilbert interrupted, "We have very little time and we cannot sleep in the forest. Please give me your money belts. Each of you must push a bicycle to the road, but we cannot all travel together."

All the money was handed to our organizer.

"Marie, you take her." Gilbert pointed at me. "Laurent, you take that one."

He held Cécile's arm and Laurent showed Diane the way to go.

Madeleine carried my clothes suitcase while I carried my transmitter.

I looked in the distance out of the woods and felt an eerie sensation run through my body, as I thought, *Now we are within the enemy's reach.* I followed Madeleine as she searched for the hidden bicycles. After she found them, we pushed our way to a road in the ghostly glow of the moon.

Madeleine spoke in a low voice the entire way out of the woods toward the road. "We must go slow and speak in whispers; we do not want any of the farmers' animals alerting anyone. Any sudden animal noise can be a death trap."

Up ahead was a body of water. "Stay away from the river because it can present our silhouettes to potential awaiting snipers. You never know when German patrols are out with their dogs. We will have to avoid direct routes the best we can. Kitty, try to lift your feet while taking short steps and push your bicycle carefully out of the woods."

"Jeanette," I corrected.

"Let's stop here in these woods. It's nice and quiet. We don't want to arrive in Paris too soon. We'd stand out and look too conspicuous." Madeleine reached into the basket of her bicycle under my suitcase and laid out wrapped food and a thermos flask on the ground.

The sky was sprinkled with twinkling stars and the woods were bathed in a misty-blue, brilliant moonlight. We ate sandwiches and drank some wine from the thermos while enjoying the radiant moon high above us.

"I was able to find some French chocolate for you."

"Chocolate? I haven't had chocolate in ages. How thoughtful of you." I savored every bite, and melted it in my mouth to enjoy the flavor. I looked at Madeleine, admiring her newly dyed red hair. I felt oddly comfortable in this occupied land, happy to be with my old roommate.

"How far are we from Paris?"

"We are 300 kilometers away and we'll have to bike to get to the city of Angers and take a train in order to get to Paris. I want you to know that the members of the Prosper circuit are glad to have you. They have found that women are less conspicuous than men." Madeleine took a sip of wine from the flask.

"*Pourquoi?*"

"Women are expected to be out shopping or doing daily chores. They are less likely to be questioned by the Gestapo than men. Besides, women are not usually searched and can hide messages in their underwear. Tell me, Jeanette, what you have been doing since I last saw you?" Madeleine inquired, touching my hand with affection.

I told her about my mission to Washington, almost wanting to confide in her about my infidelity, but felt too awkward about it. "Have you gotten any word about how Jacqueline is doing?"

"All I know is that she is in Paris, but you will find, as I have, that being a transmitter is a lonely job and we don't have much physical contact with any other agents."

Madeleine rose and put the wrappings and thermos back in her basket. As we again made our way through the woods, we stopped off and on to listen to our surroundings.

"Wait, I think I hear something. Do you have a pistol on you?"

I felt under the waistband of my skirt and nodded.

My heart pumped until Madeleine broke the silence. "*Non,* I guess it's the wind."

We reached a country road, and pedaled single-file toward the Angers railway station in the misty dawn. We left our bikes at a residence Madeleine called a "sympathizer's house," then walked to the railway station to get to Paris.

Before approaching the station, Madeleine pulled me behind a sign. "Here's your ticket. We must not sit together. One shot agent is bad enough, but two is a terrible loss."

We traveled in different compartments of the train. I glanced sideways at the people surrounding me. There were many German soldiers, which put me on edge, so I kept my eyes down toward the floor of the train. The sound of the German language made odd clipped noises, almost the opposite of the smooth, fluid sound of French. I thought back to my class at Beaulieu and remembered the photos of the German officers' uniforms presented to us. I was able to identify a few on the train. Their uniforms reminded me of that terrible night of the mock interrogation. Madeleine had been such a comfort afterward. I heard some French being spoken, and saw a few women with shopping baskets, which was somewhat calming to me. The train wound through the woods. I looked out toward the rolling fields in the dim light, which relaxed me into a much-needed sleep after the tension of arriving in occupied France.

A few hours later, Madeleine sat behind me and tapped me awake. She leaned toward the back of my seat. "We're almost there. Remember, follow close behind me until we're out of the station." She continued to speak to me in French, adding that from now on to leave the English language behind and to remember to call her Marie.

I answered in a low voice, keeping my eyes straight ahead. "Remember to call me Jeanette." I rubbed my eyes, got out a béret that Madeleine had brought me, and fixed it at an angle on my hair before stepping off the train.

Chapter 37
Occupied Paris

Paris almost looked like it had during my college days, with cafés full of people and locals going to work. Then I heard the mix of the German language and French in the street, reminding me it was not the same. Housewives were jamming into a bakery, trying like mad to get the rationed bread that would soon run out.

We continued walking together toward Rue Erlanger. There were swastikas flying from government-occupied buildings and German signs on the road. I saw rickshaw-type vehicles going by.

"*Qu'est-ce que c'est?*" I asked Madeleine.

"They're called *vélo-taxis*. There are fewer cars on the streets now because of the scarcity of petrol."

I noticed a few Mercedes zooming around carrying Nazi officials. Madeleine told me most of the people in vehicles were on official business, like police, doctors, and of course, the Germans.

When we got to the brick building displaying number 46, there were a few obvious prostitutes milling about. Madeleine and I kept our eyes down, entered the building, and took the lift to the fourth floor.

Alone in the elevator, Madeleine said, "There has been no dearth of black-market shops and restaurants in Paris for the rich, and the *métros* still run until the curfew at midnight. The Paris fashion houses are still catering for the Parisian elite and the German officers' wives. Before the war the French would say '*sales Boches*'—dirty Germans. Now all you hear is '*sales Anglais*'—dirty English." Madeleine shook her head in disgust.

"It seems like Paris has fallen without a struggle."

"You're right about that, and the Vichy government was handing over Jewish children before the Germans even asked for them. There are no more yellow stars walking around. Paris has been emptied of Jews and the Nazis have seized their vacant apartments. My family left in time under a sky full of bombing airplanes. I want my old France back."

I touched Madeleine's hand. "We'll do everything we can. How many radio operators do we have here?"

"I was the first and then there were more sent in. The SOE found that women master the keys better than men because we are adept at knitting. Not that I've ever knitted. A wireless transmitter operator has a very valuable job, as we provide the one link between London and France, but I'm afraid there are not as many 'pianists' as there were before."

Madeleine knocked on number 10 and whispered in French the code phrase through the door. "I have come on behalf of your friend

Pierre for news on the building society."

A tall man with a Basque béret opened the door. "The business is at hand."

This must be François Guyot, head of the Prosper circuit that Madeleine told me about, I thought.

He led us into the living room to sit down. He remained standing. "How are you, Marie? Tell me about the new agent you've brought."

She answered, "This is Kitty—I mean, Jeanette. She has arrived from London and is the new operator we've been expecting."

"Marie, I've told you before you'd better get your names straight. A simple, small mistake like that and you could be killed!" His eyes seemed to bulge out, exploding with anger.

She looked down and fiddled with her hands.

Monsieur Guyot turned toward me. "I hope you've brought a wireless set. They're becoming very scarce." He gave me a hard stare.

I held it up. *"Oui,* I have one with me."

"Bon. Here's the address of the new safe house you'll be staying in. Garry, the head of the Cinnema, a subcircuit of Prosper, is waiting for you." Monsieur Guyot gave Madeleine a small piece of paper and opened the door to show us out. *"Bon chance."* He locked the door after we left.

The safe house in Grignon was 21 miles from Paris, a convenient location for many of the agents to transmit from. The flat was owned by Madame Latour, a sympathizer for our cause.

After the correct passwords were exchanged through the door, Madame welcomed us in with a warm smile. "I will prepare some tea." She poked wisps of gray hair back into her bun.

"Let me help you." Madeleine followed her into the kitchen.

In the living room I met Garry, the head of the Cinnema circuit. "Have you brought a transmitter with you?"

"Oui."

"Dieu merci! They are beginning to get quite scarce because, I am sorry to say, the Nazis have been very successful in seizing them, as well

as our operators. Our circuit is happy to add you. Let me brief you. There are about 400 FANY operators in Grendon, England, manning radio sets, but not enough people here to even transmit. Our main circuit, Prosper, has been responsible for the destruction of over 1,000 litres of petrol and derailing enemy trains carrying valuable goods. We have found 33 dropping zones and received over 150 containers. Jeanette, welcome to Paris. We're happy to have a much-needed transmitter such as yourself."

"I'm glad to be able to help the cause." I gave him a slight smile.

Madeleine carried a tea tray and placed it on a table adorned with a crocheted tablecloth. Madame Latour put a plate of sliced bread next to it. Madeleine proceeded to pour milk into the four teacups from a small white pitcher, then added the hot tea from the pot.

Garry burst into a rage. *"Zut alors!* Why are you pouring milk into the cups before the tea?" He jabbed his finger toward the tea tray.

Madeleine, who had just taken a sip of her tea, rattled her cup down on her saucer. "Uh, I forgot."

I covered my mouth with my hand. I knew that pouring milk into the cups before the tea was an English custom—a dead giveaway in France.

Madeleine apologized again, but I noticed she did not take another sip.

Garry gave us our daily "skeds," which was the frequency and time used to come on the air. He also gave us a message to transmit back to England. "Don't forget to memorize them, then burn." His sharp gray eyes caught Madeleine's for a moment and he left without another word.

Madeleine looked at the schedules. "I have five minutes to set up. Come help me."

Madame Latour showed us our room, up the stairs. The Mark II needed 70 feet of aerial, which made it very conspicuous. I leaned out the window, throwing it around an overgrown chestnut tree the best I could. Madeleine took the scrap of paper that Garry had given her, plugged the power lead into an electrical outlet, and turned on the power switch.

After she was done setting up, she told me, "It's very important that we keep our transmissions short, 10-15 minutes. I've been told if you don't keep it brief, the German Direction Finding vans will come for you at your doorstep within a half an hour. They are disguised as bakery or laundry vans and are constantly circling the streets." Madeleine proceeded to transmit. After she finished, she latched the suitcase, closing the transmitter, then got out a portfolio from a desk drawer and put the transmission information in it.

I got the aerial out of the tree and wrapped it up.

"There are many precautions we must take. We both have to keep moving because of the German listening devices. Tomorrow you will be given your own assignment and we will have to part."

"*Merci* for helping me, Marie. I will do my best for France."

As we lay in our beds that night, Madeleine told me about enlisting the help of a German soldier the previous week. She was outside trying to put the antenna up into the tree when the soldier came by, asking her what she was doing. Recognizing his plain uniform, she said she was stringing up a clothesline for her laundry and asked if he could help her. This tactic worked, but she added that she decided she had better install it from upstairs from then on.

I had very little to say after hearing about that. Sleep did not come well to me. I began to feel quite worried about my friend. She seemed rather negligent in her ways, from calling me the wrong name to the tea incident. Now she had told me about a close encounter with a German soldier. At least she had been able to cover up that mistake. For such an intelligent, knowledgeable person, she was prone to constant slip-ups. I tossed and turned until morning.

Chapter 38
Marie

We went downstairs, where Madame Latour had prepared a simple but delicious breakfast for us.

Her husband came in with a folder in his hands. *"Bonjour, Mesdemoiselles.* Does this belong to one of you?" He held up Madeleine's portfolio.

"Merci." Madeleine's face flushed and she took it from him.

My mouth fell open with surprise. "Oh…" I covered it in astonishment, wondering how she could have left out her folder that contained all her security codes. At Beaulieu, we were told to never keep written transmissions around. We were taught various tricks to hide them, such as writing on thin tissue or rice paper, then stuffing the messages into cigarettes. They could also be eaten if necessary, but should never be kept on a permanent basis.

We made our way back to Monsieur François Guyot's place to get our daily schedules, or skeds, along with any messages that needed to be transmitted to London. I noticed a Gestapo officer on the corner tapping his ear, and assumed he must have a miniature listening set. The officer glanced over at me and I pointed at a store window saying in French to Madeleine, "What a lovely dress. I wish we had the money to buy one."

After the password was exchanged, Monsieur Guyot opened the door and looked out past us in case we had been followed. "Marie, have you found a new place to transmit from?"

Madeleine answered, *"Oui,* I found a flat where my old music teacher from college, Yvette Damerment, lives."

François interrupted her. "I do not want that much information. *Oui ou non*, would have been sufficient." He faced me. "Jeanette, you will have to go out on your own now. On this paper is a new safe house for you to transmit from and here are your own skeds. From now on, I want you both to get your skeds from Balignani bookstore on Rue Vivienne, at different times. The password to receive them is also on the paper." He handed me a small note, shielding it from Madeleine, adding, "Memorize and destroy." Next, Guyot gave me two different numbered crystals. "Here are your crystals. They're very delicate even though they are surrounded by bakelite. They will break if dropped. Be careful with them. They've been very hard to replace."

I placed the skeds and crystals deep into my coat pocket.

"And here are yours, Marie." He held out her crystals and skeds. She placed the crystals in her jumper pocket and the skeds in a portfolio.

"What is that folder for?" Guyot's voice boomed.

"My portfolio."

"What do you have in there?"

"I file all my codes, frequencies, and transmitting times."

"*O, mon Dieu!* This is extremely dangerous. If the Germans got ahold of all the codes they could pretend they are you and infiltrate the entire circuit." Guyot crossed his arms; his face turned red.

"But I carry it around in order to not leave it anywhere," Madeleine declared with self-confidence.

"You know you are supposed to destroy all your past messages."

"*Non,* London told me to file them."

"That is not correct. You must always destroy all your past messages. Do you understand?" Now his arms were shaking.

Madeleine nodded and looked toward the door.

We both left and walked a few blocks together.

"Marie, please try to be more careful. I am very worried about you."

"It doesn't matter. I will continue to help my country. If the Germans catch me, they can do what they like with me, but they will *never* get anything out of me."

Further worry consumed me about my close friend.

We were both reluctant to part ways and embraced with a fierce tenderness.

Madeleine whispered in my ear, "May God keep you."

I fought back my tears. "And you, as well."

A week went by, during which I was able to develop a routine by staying with a distinguished biologist, his wife, and two small sons. They lived in a small house at the National College of Agriculture. I was able to transmit and receive from the greenhouse while the gardener kept watch. After I was done, I hid my set in a cabbage patch.

The next day I went to my assigned cachette. The bookstore on Rue Vivienne was very old, its date of 1801 carved on the thick, dark door. Madeleine told me they were strictly ordered by the Germans to stop selling and stocking English editions.

"Do you have any *Madame Bovary* by Flaubert in stock?" I asked, using the given code phrase.

The young storekeeper answered, *"Oui,* a volume has just come in." He went into the back and brought me a copy. If he had said, "We are out of stock," that would have meant there were no messages that day.

"Merci." I paid him and left.

At the garden, I retrieved my Mark II and went into the greenhouse. I opened the book to page 77 and there was a thin piece of rice paper with all the pertinent information on it. I placed my daytime crystal in the transmitter, being very careful with it.

The next day, I received a message from London at the designated time. The transmission ended with "May God keep you." I knew it was from Miss Armstrong and smiled, remembering those were her last words to me before I had left in the Lysander. I thought of Madeleine using the same phrase, and prayed she was safe.

I brought the message to my designated Dead Letter Box on 23 Rue des Bernardins, placing it in a hole in the wall of Eglise Saint-Nicolas-du-Chardonnet, a 17th-century church. The message read to expect two Canadian agents.

The following week, I went to my Dead Letter Box and felt a paper when I was putting my message deep inside the crack in the wall. I took out the message before putting in mine, and stuffed it into my coat pocket, then proceeded back to the college.

In the greenhouse I read, *Come by for a visit as soon as possible. — F. G.*

I went to François Guyot's residence. I wondered why he would risk exposure by having me come by. I looked all around me before knocking on the door. After exchanging passwords, I was let inside.

Guyot wasted no time telling me the news. "The two Canadians never showed up. One of their parachutes came down on a tree and a suitcase burst open, spilling clothes on the branches. One container exploded, which alerted the nearby Germans. The Canadian agents were caught on the road with uncoded messages for many of our agents in the Prosper circuit. The Germans now have all the safe house addresses. Furthermore, two twin sisters, Ginette and Odette, were captured and were sent to Fresnes prison. I have been negotiating their exchange for one million francs with a German colonel in Paris. Prosper circuit is now too large with too many sub-circuits that have been infiltrated. I have been advised by London to stop the negotiations because many agents were arrested in the process. I am sorry to say, the Germans have arrested most of the circuit." Guyot took a nervous breath and continued, "Marie has received a transmission from headquarters telling all radio operators to go back home before it's too late. I must also relocate. I need you to go back to the college and bring me your Mark II. Marie has arranged for a Lysander tonight that you must leave on at 1600 hours."

My mouth opened but nothing came out of it.

"What are you waiting for? GO!"
"Uh…uh…what about Marie?"
"Don't ask."

Chapter 39
Escape

I went back and could see from a distance that the greenhouse had been smashed. I was tempted to look through the cabbage patch, but thought better of it and left. I felt my lapel. I was comforted that I had put on my silver bird from Officer Armstrong. The rest of my belongings were now gone.

A German officer asked for my passport when I was about to board the train to Angers. I handed it to him. He thumbed through every page, then he looked me over for what felt like a long time. I forced a smile and unbuttoned my top button, which distracted him. He shoved the passport back to me, which allowed me to board the train. The ride was a fearful one. I tried to maintain my composure and went to the lavatory to wipe my sweaty face.

I got off at Angers, and strolled as slow as I could away from the train station. Thank God a bicycle was still hidden on the side of the cottage where Madeleine and I had left them only a few weeks ago.

As I biked along the road, every time I heard a vehicle I veered off into the woods and didn't come back out until it was gone. At last, I recognized the farmer's house and left my bike near a tree, then proceeded with caution toward the field. I heard some voices, and stopped to listen, but I did not hear any German spoken and continued on.

There waiting to escape were Jacqueline, Cécile, and Diane. They all kissed me.

Jacqueline asked me urgently, "Have you seen Madeleine?"

"I was hoping she would be here."

We heard the Lysander and I looked out toward the woods, but I knew it would be too late now for her to make it.

The flight back on the Lysander was nothing like the one getting to Angers. Sure, there was the same nervousness, like persistent static electricity, but this time the pilot was an obvious visible wreck. He didn't say anything the entire four-hour flight, but kept slugging away from his flask of alcohol.

We arrived in Tangmere, and I felt weary and disoriented. I staggered down the ladder onto the tarmac. From a distance in front of the hangar, I could see someone waving. Officer Armstrong greeted all the returning agents and came up to me last. I grabbed her with all my might, exhausted with emotion.

After we embraced, she touched my collar. "You still have my silver bird, Kathleen, and I see that it did bring you good luck."

It was soothing to hear my real name and I began to feel more at ease.

No one spoke in the station wagon on the way back to London. Our mental resources were gone like dirty water down a washtub drain.

Miss Armstrong showed us to our rooms above her office. I fell fast asleep.

The next morning in her office, Miss Armstrong greeted us. "You all escaped right on time. Prosper has fallen completely apart. Thank God Madeleine was able to transmit to have a plane sent for all of you." Miss Armstrong told us all the horrific details about the fall of Prosper.

"What about Marie…I mean, Madeleine?" My heart pounded.

"When will she return?" Jacqueline demanded.

Officer Armstrong shuffled papers on her desk. "Guyot arrived this morning and told me Madeleine refused to leave because she knew she had the only transmitter left that had not been seized by the Germans."

"She refused to leave?"

"Yes. Madeleine was an agent with many faults, but her bravery is second to none. Guyot said she was determined to continue to work with the French Resistance to try to rebuild the Prosper circuit with local contacts."

"Have you heard from her?" I demanded.

"No, I'm afraid not."

"Can you tell me how my daughter is?" Jacqueline inquired.

"She's doing well with your mother and you should go home to join them."

Diane and Cécile received details about their families.

I burst out, "What about my husband?"

Miss Armstrong looked down to rearrange her papers to avoid my face. "He was shot in Sicily, but survived and is recuperating at your house."

"Shot?"

"I'm afraid so, but he is alive. I will arrange a troop ship for you to go back home and inform your husband to meet you." Miss Armstrong handed me the uncensored letter from Fred.

> *Kathleen, my dearest:*
>
> *Operation Husky proved to be a very difficult mission. We were towed in the middle of the night through fierce headwinds and saw searchlights, then heard enemy gunners fire below. I witnessed six C-47s plunge into the sea.*
>
> *Through my radio, I shouted to our tow plane not to cut us loose in the Mediterranean Sea below. We were never trained what to do upon landing in water. Even though there were lifejackets on board, we knew we could die of hypothermia.*

While descending on Sicily, pieces of another glider above us fell on ours after it was shot down. We kept right on flying, hoping the enemy would run out of ammunition. The fog made the accuracy of landing very difficult.

Once on the ground, there before us was a carpet of gliders that had landed. When I was searching about, I found one of our pilots burned to a crisp still behind his controls. I identified him by his dog tags, and tore them off in order to report back that he had died. This was quite a frightening experience for me to witness.

Out of nowhere, two Italian soldiers rushed toward me and before I could pull out my gun, shot my co-pilot dead. I yelled out in agony, watching him die, but kept quiet after they shot my leg. When I was being held captive, British officers came upon us and took the Italians as prisoners.

I will write more later, if I have the strength.

All my love, Fred

"My poor husband, what he has gone through." I choked and tried to hold back my tears. "I guess this means my service is over now."

"You have all been outstanding agents and will not be forgotten. Let's all stay in touch." Vivian Armstrong went to get all our boxes.

When Vivian returned, I tried to remove her silver brooch, but she refused. "No, it's yours now. Who knows? It may bring you further good luck in the future."

During my long journey home on the troop ship, I tried to sort out my past life. I felt unsettled and defeated, like a pitcher in the middle of a baseball game that suddenly got rained out. I didn't like leaving

Madeleine behind.

I would lie in my berth, or go out on the upper deck in the dark for long breaths of sea air. I began to travel back in time in my mind.

I reflected on my beginnings at Camp X, Beaulieu finishing school, then Washington, D.C. This led me to thoughts about my husband. I thought about the genuine kindness he showed toward Mom and the understanding he displayed in his letters. I was very grateful that Fred was alive and was looking forward to holding him in my arms…but was deeply worried he would sense my infidelity. I had betrayed him while he was risking his life in a plane without an engine.

Fred met me at the pier in New York City and was gripping a cane. I sobbed and held him while his thin body shook.

"You're alive," I said, and he repeated the same back to me. He shared his shock of learning from Miss Armstrong that I had been an intelligence agent.

We were both lost in silence on the long bus ride to Rochester. Would we ever be able to settle into a routine back at home after all we had been through?

Chapter 40
Two Years Later

Lamb! I selected the finest ingredients at the store for an intimate dinner with my husband. *He will be quite surprised when he comes home tonight from the factory.* It was a joy to buy everything without having to worry about those difficult ration coupons. I balanced the shopping bag of food in the crook of one arm and reached into the mailbox. An envelope. It was rare these days for me to receive a letter.

11/1/45

Dear Kathleen:

Thank the Good Lord that this long, arduous war is over. I hope this letter finds you well. I know you were quite close to Madeleine, and I wanted to report back to you about her.

I have been spending my time taking up the task of finding out what has happened to all my girls who never returned from the field. I have traveled to Germany and have been successful in interviewing many German officers.

Yes, Madeleine was captured and did pass away in prison, but I wanted to reassure you that she left this earth not passively, but fighting for her beloved country.

Madeleine refused to return to England when you did because she knew she was the only remaining radio link between France and England. After you left occupied France, between 400-1,500 members of the Resistance were arrested. Madeleine was able to perform the work of six radio operators as other heads of circuits started asking her to transmit for them. She sent messages to London to request arms, explosives, and money needed by the French Resistance. London sent her many details about parachute drops in order for the Resistance to retrieve needed goods. Madeleine facilitated the escape of 30 Allied airmen that had been shot down in France.

Occupied Paris began to get more and more dangerous. There were Gestapo everywhere and she became their most hunted animal. The Prosper circuit had become too big, allowing it to be infiltrated by the Germans.

Madeleine had rented a room that was, unbeknownst to her, surrounded by Nazi soldiers living there, and was opposite the headquarters of the Gestapo. A French officer, whom I was able to interview, worked for the Gestapo and arrested Madeleine. This officer told me she struggled with violence, and even bit him, drawing blood. He called her a fighting "tigeress." The Gestapo arrived and seized her transmitter, along with her portfolio, exposing all her codes.

Once the Germans seized her wireless set, they could send false information to the SOE in London by posing as Madeleine. They sent messages for more men to be sent into France and these additional agents were captured. The smashing of the Prosper network led to the infiltration of another.

I was able to uncover the fact that Guyot's sister, Renée, betrayed Madeleine. At the Gestapo headquarters Renée told Officer Kieffer that she would tell them where Madeleine was if she was paid 100,000 francs. They gave Renée half the money for a full description along with Madeleine's address, and then would give her the other half when Madeleine was arrested.

The SOE suspects that François Guyot was a double agent and he is under investigation.

Madeleine was classified by the Nazis as a dangerous

prisoner and was put in solitary confinement in Pforzheim prison in Germany. The prison records showed that she was discharged after a year and transferred to Dachau, where she was given the full treatment of torture, then shot.

Kitty, I'm sure you feel as upset as I am after reading this account of our brave Madeleine. It is also sad to note that seven months after she was killed, Dachau was liberated. I am recommending Madeleine to the head of the SOE for the Croix de Guerre with Gold Star, including the George Cross for her bravery and devotion to duty despite the collapse of her circuit.

I hope all is well with your husband and please keep in touch.

Fondly, Vivian Armstrong

I folded the letter back into the envelope and gently touched the silver bird on my blouse. I rocked for a while in my dad's old oak rocking chair. I rubbed my hard, round abdomen, thinking my brother's name would be good for a boy…and Madeleine if I had a girl.

EPILOGUE

While women are still officially not allowed in combat in most nations, there is a long history of female involvement in warfare. Espionage knows no gender, and in fact, being a female provides less suspicion with a better cover.

American women spies during World War II include: Josephine Baker, Mary Bancroft, Virginia Hall, Claire Phillips, Elizabeth Reynolds, and Elizabeth Amy Thorpe (Betty Pack).

7/22/1940: Special Operations Executive (SOE) was established to coordinate subversive and sabotage activity against the enemy. It had three chiefs: Sir Frank Nelson, Sir Charles Hambro, and Major General Colin Gubbins.

The SOE sent 480 agents into France to fight the Nazis; 53 were women, and 15 died.

There were 50 SOE training establishments in Britain.

The total number of men and women trained by SOE was approximately 13,000.

In Britain there were 6,800 students (most were nationals of enemy-occupied countries) who took 13,500 courses provided by the SOE.

A total of 812 students were trained in parachute jumping at Ringway Airfield, Manchester, England.

6/13/1942: The Office of Strategic Services (OSS), a United States intelligence agency, was established. Head of the office: William J. "Wild Bill" Donovan. There were approximately 30,000 in the agency.

The OSS was formed in order to coordinate espionage activities behind enemy lines for the branches of the United States Armed Forces.

The first OSS agents were trained by British Security Coordination (BSC) in Canada, until training stations were set up in the United States with guidance from BSC instructors, who also provided information on how the SOE was arranged and managed. The British immediately made available their short-wave broadcasting capabilities to Europe, Africa, and the Far East, and provided equipment for agents until American production was established.

There were many Special Training Schools all over the world for training spies during WW II. In addition to traditional spies, these organizations employed many ordinary men and women to covertly provide information about strategic locations and activities while leading normal lives. The SOE was active in virtually every occupied country in Europe, aiding the Resistance groups and monitoring enemy activity, and also had operatives in the enemy countries themselves. The American counterpart overlapped some of the SOE operations and also had operatives in the Pacific theater. The OSS became the current CIA.

Biographies

of

Real

World War II

Spies

Virginia Hall
4/1906 - 7/8/1982

Virginia Hall was an American spy with the SOE, OSS and CIA. In the SOE she helped coordinate the activities of the French Underground in Vichy.

November, 1942: Hiked on foot through the Pyrenees Mountains into Spain when the Germans seized France. Before making her escape, she signaled to SOE that she hoped "Cuthbert" (her nickname for her false leg from a hunting accident) would not give her trouble on the way. The SOE, not understanding the reference, replied, "If Cuthbert troublesome, eliminate him!"

She joined the OSS, and was sent back to France disguised as an old peasant woman. She was responsible for the killing and capture of hundreds of German soldiers, as well as sabotaging communications and transportation links. She trained three battalions of Resistance forces, located drop zones for money and weapons, found safe houses, and helped escaped prisoners of war and Allied airmen flee to France. The Germans had a reward out for her capture. They called her "the limping lady" and she was on their most wanted and dangerous list. In fact, there were wanted posters all over France offering a reward for her capture.

In July of 1943, journeying back to London (after working for SOE for a time in Madrid), she was quietly made a Member of the Order of the British Empire. In September of 1945, she was awarded the Distinguished Service Cross, which was the only one awarded to a civilian woman in World War II. She was America's most decorated female agent in France.

Elizabeth Amy Thorpe (Betty Pack)
11/22/1910 - 12/1/1963

Sir William Samuel Stephenson of the British Security Coordination recruited her to gather intelligence due to her wide network of contacts. She used her sexual prowess to complete her missions.

She volunteered with the British as a spy and obtained the flow of Polish intelligence on the German Enigma code to Britain.

In May, 1941, disguised as a freelance writer, she met Charles Brousse, French press attaché in Washington, D.C. and obtained the Vichy French Naval ciphers. There was no way of knowing what value stealing the French Naval codes played; it is thought that it assisted the Allied invasion of North Africa.

Noor Inayat Khan
1/2/1914 - 9/13/1944

She was the first female radio operator sent by Britain to occupied France to aid the French Resistance. She was also a direct descendant of Tipu Sultan, the 18th-century Muslim ruler of Mysore, and her father, Hazrat Inayat Khan, was a Sufi teacher. Her family escaped to England after the fall of France.

On November 19, 1940, she joined the Women's Auxiliary Air Force and trained as a wireless operator.

February, 1943: Joined the SOE as a radio operator.

June 16, 1943: Was flown into France to become a radio operator for the Prosper Resistance network in Paris. She remained in France after most of the members of the network were arrested to continue transmitting messages to London.

October 13, 1943: Noor was betrayed by someone and was arrested, interrogated, and taken to Gestapo headquarters. Although she remained silent, they discovered a book in her possession where she had recorded all her messages. The Gestapo was able to break her code, sent false information to the SOE in London, and captured three more secret agents that landed in France. Noor was interrogated, was able to escape, but was recaptured.

On November 26, 1943, Noor was taken to Nazi Germany where she was imprisoned at Pforzheim in solitary confinement. For 10 months she was kept there, classified as "highly dangerous," and shackled in chains most of the time. As the prison director testified after the war, Noor Inayat Khan remained uncooperative and continued to refuse to give any information on her work or her fellow operatives.

September 13, 1944: Noor was moved to the Dachau Concentration

Camp where she was shot in the head with four other women at age 30.

January 16, 1946: Noor Inayat Khan was posthumously awarded by General Charles De Gaulle, France's highest civilian award, the Croix de Guerre with Gold Star.

April 4, 1949: England awarded her the George Cross.

There are memorials in Dachau Concentration Camp and Grignon.

A square in Suresnes, France has been named "Cours Madeleine" after her. Every year on Bastille Day, July 14, a military band plays tribute to her there.

November 8, 2012: The Noor Inayat Khan Memorial was installed in Gordon Square, England, unveiled by Princess Anne.

Vera Atkins
6/16/1908 - 6/24/2000

In February of 1941, she became an intelligence officer of the French section of the SOE. Atkins recruited and deployed mostly female agents.

When the Allied victory in Europe was accomplished, she went to Germany. As a member of the British War Crimes Commission, she investigated the fate of the 118 F section agents who had disappeared in enemy territory. After a year visiting concentration camps and interrogating the German guards, she established how and when the missing agents had perished. She succeeded in every case except one.

Atkins displayed formidable skills as an interrogator. Hugo Bleicher, the Abwehr officer who had wreaked havoc among the French Resistance, judged her interrogation the most skillful to which he had been subjected by his captors.

In March of 1946 she also interrogated Rudolf Hoess, the German Commandant of Auschwitz, who had been living disguised as a farmer. When asked whether it was true that he had caused the deaths of 1.5 million Jews, he indignantly protested that this was wrong: the real figure was 2,345,000.

In 1987, Atkins was appointed Commandant of the Legion of Honor.

Bibliography

Basu, Shrabani. *Spy Princess, The Life of Noor Inayat Khan.* Sheridan Books, Sutton Publishing Ltd. London, England. 2006.

Binney, Marcus. *The Women Who Lived For Danger.* Hodder & Stoughton, London, England. 2002.

Breuer, William B. *The Spy Who Spent the War in Bed.* John Wiley & Sons, Inc., Hoboken, NJ. 2003.

Breuer, William B. *Top Secret Tales of World War II.* John Wiley & Sons, Inc. Hoboken, New Jersey. 2000.

Belanger, Joe. *Catalina Island.* Roundtable Publishing, Mesa, AZ. 2000.

Cunningham, Cyril. *Beaulieu. The Finishing School for Secret Agents.* Pen & Sword Books, Ltd., South Yorkshire, England. 1998.

Devlin, Gerard M. *Paratrooper! The Saga of US Army and Marine Parachute and Glider Combat Troops During World War II.* St. Martin's Press, NY. 1979.

Devlin, Gerard M. *Silent Wings.* St. Martin's Press, N.Y. 1985.

Blum, Stella, ed. *Everyday Fashions of the Forties, as Pictured in Sears Catalogs.* Dover Publications, Inc. NY, NY. 1986.

Foot, MRD. *SOE in France.* Staples Printers Limited, Kent, England. 1966.

Helm, Sarah. *A Life in Secrets, Vera Atkins and the Missing Agents of WW II.* Doubleday Publishing Group. NY, NY. 2005.

Hodgson, Lynn Philip. *Inside Camp X.* Blake Book Distribution, Ontario, Canada. 2002.

Hyde, H. Montgomery. *The Quiet Canadian, The Secret Service Story of Sir William Stephenson.* Constable & Co. Limited, London, England. 1962.

Lovell, Mary S. *Cast No Shadow, The Life of the American Spy Who Changed the Course of World War II.* Random House. Toronto, Canada. 1992.

McIntosh, Elizabeth. *Sisterhood of Spies.* Dell Publishing, NY. 1998.

Melton, H. Keith. *The Ultimate Spy Book.* DK Publishing, Inc., NY, NY. 1996.

Miller, Russell. *Behind The Lines, The Oral History of Special Operations in World War II.* New American Library, NY, NY. 2002.

O'Donnell, Patrick K. *Operatives, Spies, and Saboteurs.* Kennington Publishing Corp. NY, NY. 2004.

Payment, Simone. *American Women Spies of World War II.* Rosen Publishing, NY. 2004.

Pearson, Judith L. *The Wolves at the Door, The True Story of America's Greatest Female Spy.* Globe Pequot Press, Guilford, CT, 2005.

Pedersen, Jeannine. *Catalina Island.* Arcadia Publishing, Charleston SC. 2004.

Rigden, Denis (introduction). *How to be a Spy, The World War II SOE Training Manual,* published in arrangement with The National Archive, UK. Durndurn Press, Toronto, Canada. 2001.

Stafford, David. *Camp X.* Dodd, Mead & Company. NY, NY. 1986.

Stevenson, William. *A Man Called Intrepid.* Harcourt, Brace, Jovanovich, NY. 1976.

Stevenson, William. *Spymistress.* Arcade Publishing, Inc. NY, NY. 2007.

Sullivan, George. *In the Line of Fire, Eight Women War Spies.* Scholastic Inc. NY, NY. 1966.

Verity, Hugh. *We Landed by Moonlight, The Secret RAF Landings in France 1940-1944.* Crecy Publishing Limited, England. 2000.

Walters, Eric. *Camp X.* Penguin, Toronto, Canada. 2002.

White, William Sanford. *Santa Catalina Island Goes to War, World War II, 1941-1945.* White Limited Editions, Glendora, CA. 2002.

About the Front Cover

"Les Marguerites Fleuriront Ce Soir"
(The Daisies Will Bloom Tonight)
A painting of WW II OSS spy Virginia Hall by artist Jeffery Bass

On 6/6/1944, Virginia Hall was directed by OSS headquarters in London to travel to the province of Auvergne to organize a Resistance circuit. She stayed on the Lebrat farm, which provided refuge for members of the Resistance. The message, *"les marguerites fleuriront ce soir,"* was typical of the coded messages that Virginia monitored on BBC broadcasts, alerting her to expect an airdrop at a specific time and place.

In this painting, Virginia Hall is sending a radio transmission to London from the Lebrat's quaint, fieldstone barn on her British SOE Type 3, Mark II suitcase transmitter. Edmond Lebrat, a Resistance fighter, assisted Virginia by providing an electrical power source improvised from an old bicycle and an automobile generator.

Jeffrey Bass is a fine art portrait painter and commercial artist. His works include a portrait of President George H.W. Bush. This painting of Virginia Hall is displayed in the CIA as part of its fine arts collection in Washington, D.C.

About the Author

Photo by Star Dewar

Jeane Slone is the past Vice President and a present board member of the California Redwood Writer's Club, a member of the Healdsburg Literary Guild, the Military Writer's Society of America, and the Pacific Coast Air Museum. Ms. Slone is also the host of the television show "Writer/Speak," and is a tutor for the Library Literary Program.

Ms. Slone has published the historical fictions *She Flew Bombers* (winner of the national 2012 Indie Book Award), and *She Built Ships During WW II*.

Jeane Slone enjoys researching pieces of the forgotten past, especially involving female heroines and multi-cultures.

Ms. Slone's hands-on experience to complete *She Was an American Spy During World War II* included: skydiving, shooting a WW II Colt .45, and use of a 1948 clandestine RS-1 HF transceiver. She also viewed authentic spy displays at The Military Intelligence Museum in Bedford, England, and Musée de L'Armée in Paris, France.

Visit: www.JeaneSlone.com
Email: info@jeaneslone.com

The author shooting a WW II .45 Colt

The author skydiving

Made in the USA
San Bernardino, CA
24 November 2013